Can I Get a Do-Over?

The Grace of Second Chances

Elizabeth Ward

BARBOUR
PUBLISHING

Print ISBN 978-1-61626-547-2

eBook Editions:
Adobe Digital Edition (.epub) 978-1-60742-806-0
Kindle and MobiPocket Edition (.prc) 978-1-60742-807-7

Cover illustration: Michael Anstin, theisspot.com

Published by Barbour Publishing, Inc., P.O. Box 719, Uhrichsville, Ohio 44683
www.barbourbooks.com

Our mission is to publish and distribute inspirational products offering exceptional value and biblical encouragement to the masses.

Member of the
Evangelical Christian
Publishers Association

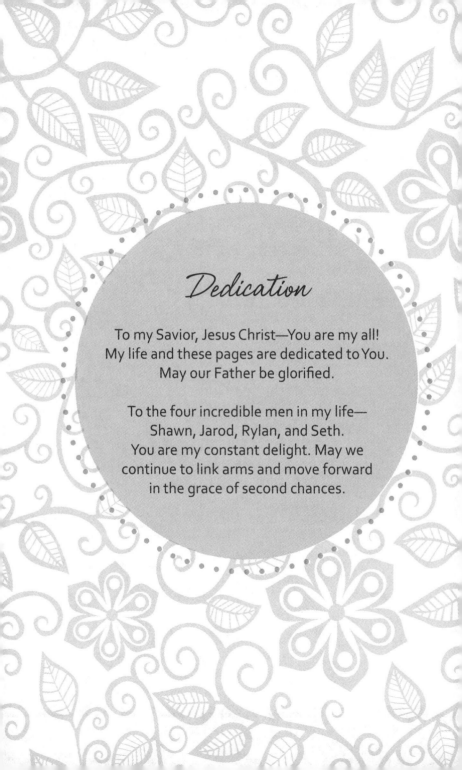

Dedication

To my Savior, Jesus Christ—You are my all!
My life and these pages are dedicated to You.
May our Father be glorified.

To the four incredible men in my life—
Shawn, Jarod, Rylan, and Seth.
You are my constant delight. May we
continue to link arms and move forward
in the grace of second chances.

Contents

Introduction

In the 1920s, Ira Yates and his wife, Ann, owned a large plot of land in Texas that they used for grazing sheep. Although Ira loved ranching, the land was dry and unfruitful, and he struggled to make a profit. A friend encouraged Ira to drill for oil despite the fact that no oil had ever been found in this barren area of Texas.

The oil company got to work and before long, it drilled an oil well that became the most lucrative oil well found on that side of the country at that time in history. Mr. Yates had become an instant millionaire. He went from being poor to rich, barren to abundant. Or had he? In actuality, Ira and Ann Yates had been millionaires all along. That resource of wealth had been theirs from the second they had obtained the land. They just didn't know it.

If you are a believer in Jesus Christ, you, like Ira Yates, have been a millionaire all along. In Christ, we have the richest resource available, and yet many of us are living life as if we are empty and feeling unfulfilled.

My grandmother had a bountiful garden every summer. Come harvesttime, she would can everything from applesauce to tomato juice, stocking up her pantry for the winter. Before canning, she would get all the jars out of storage and spend most of the day sterilizing each one. With great care, she washed each jar until it was sparkling clean. Now, what if I told you that after she spent the whole day cleaning the jars she opened the cupboard and put them all back on the shelf? She would say, "Well, that was a wonderful day of cleaning canning jars. I'm so pleased with the work that I've accomplished. I can hardly wait until next year when I can get them all out and clean them again." Seriously, what would we think of Grandma? Perhaps we'd think she had a screw loose or was a little desperate for something to occupy herself. The point is, my grandmother has way too much sense to do something like that. The only reason she goes to all that trouble to clean canning jars is because she wants to fill them up with the abundant provision of her "fruit-filled" labor.

Jesus does the same thing. Christ cleaned us once for all to fill us up with the provision of Himself. He didn't clean us to set us on the shelf until it was time to clean us again. Nor did He clean us in order to leave us empty. He has purified each jar of clay so that it might be filled with the all-surpassing power of God in Christ. Beloved, if Christ has cleaned you, He has filled you. Do you know that you are a millionaire? Do you recognize the resource you have in Christ? If not, I have good news for you! God is granting us a do-over. . .to understand a makeover. . .that is meant to take over. . .and it has everything to do with the grace of second chances. This woman needs a do-over. Won't you join me?

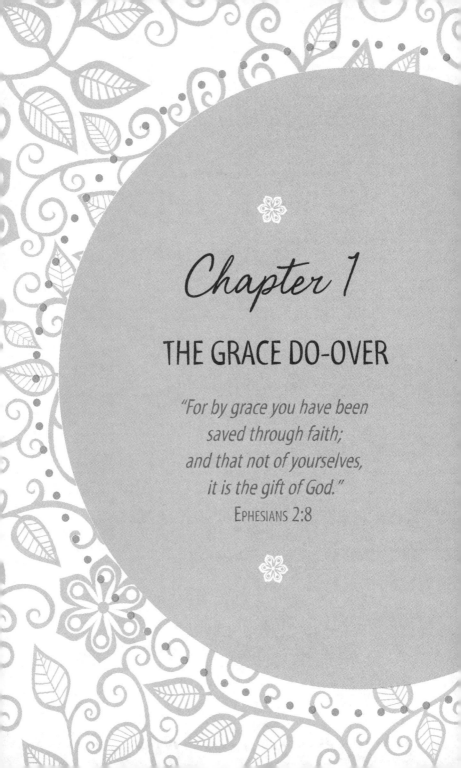

Chapter 1

THE GRACE DO-OVER

*"For by grace you have been
saved through faith;
and that not of yourselves,
it is the gift of God."*
Ephesians 2:8

"Can I have a do-over?" I heard myself say as I was looking into my friend's tear-streaked face. Just a short time ago, we had headed out to find her a dress for her approaching wedding. She had found one she liked and wanted to get my opinion. So off we went to the specialty store, where glamorous gowns decorated the large front windows. Now here she stood, in the corner of the dressing room, surrounded by mirrored walls that reflected the dress she had chosen. It was knee length, strapless, gathered at the waist, and pink with white polka dots. She stood smiling as she waited for my response.

My friend is a very attractive woman, and she looked quite nice in the dress. But our tastes are somewhat dissimilar, particularly when it comes to clothing. This particular time, I think it was the pink with polka dots that threw me. Well, I had hesitated just long enough that my friend's eyes began to fill up with tears. Of course at that point, there was no way to fill in the previous gap of silence. So I immediately began to try to put my thoughts into words, saying something like, "I like it, it looks nice." To which she responded, "It looks *nice*?" You must emphasize the "nice" in order to hear her tone. She was obviously hurt by my lack of excitement and again, the extended pause before my response. Now she was crying.

I felt absolutely horrible. I tried to console, to add additional positive elements, but there was really no way to gain what I had lost. She knew me well enough to know that I didn't think too much of the dress. Despite my ill feelings for her choice, my feelings for my friend were quite the opposite. I knew she was tired. I knew she wanted the perfect dress. I knew she valued my opinion of it. I knew this was only one of many decisions she was trying to bring to an end. And in her desire to get it all right, my hint of hesitation had pushed her over the edge emotionally. Despite my attempts to console, to encourage, to redirect, her tears continued to flow.

Now, most of us have been there. I knew that I hadn't done anything wrong, but do you ever have those times when you think, *I could have done* that *better*? I desperately longed for a do-over.

That was just one of many times in my life when I could have used a do-over. Fortunately, I'm not alone. Many men and women in the Bible could have used a do-over as well. Abram took Sarai to Egypt and lied to Pharaoh in order to save his own skin. Moses used tons of excuses as to why he couldn't deliver the Israelites. Rahab chose prostitution as her profession. The woman at the well had five husbands. Peter denied Christ three times, and Paul killed Christians.

But God, rich in the business of do-overs, "who makes a way through the sea and a path through the mighty waters" tells us, "'Do not call to mind the former things, or ponder things of the past. Behold, *I will do something new,* now it will spring forth; will you not be aware of it? I will even make a roadway in the wilderness, rivers in the desert'" (Isaiah 43:16, 18–19, emphasis added). And that's exactly what God does when we are willing to turn over our poorly done *do's* into His hands. He will take whatever we give Him—any weakness, any poor decisions, any sin confessed—and He will do something new. Our God is a God of second chances and an absolute Master at extending do-overs to those who call on His name.

Abram obeyed God and became the "father of many nations" (Romans 4:17). Moses delivered the people from captivity in the land of Egypt despite his feelings of inadequacy. Rahab is listed in the lineage of Christ in spite of her *do's.* The woman at the well finally met Jesus, the man of her dreams. Peter endlessly proclaimed Christ, and Paul planted church upon church for the kingdom of God. God offers do-overs to His people as we turn to Him! How precious is the grace of second chances! And to think, their God is our God, and He "is the same yesterday and today and forever" (Hebrews 13:8)!

Yes, our God is still in the business of do-overs, and the grace of second chances is still readily available. Are you in need of a do-over, friend? Do you need to experience the grace of second chances? The God of the Bible, Jesus Christ, is in the business of offering you a do-over that can change your life forever!

*"In [Christ] we have redemption through His blood,
the forgiveness of our trespasses according to the riches
of His grace, which He lavished on us."*

EPHESIANS 1:7–8

If you know Jesus as your Savior, then you have been
redeemed by His blood and forgiven of your sin. To
what extent? The verse above says "according to
the riches of His grace which He lavished on us." You
had a do-over that not only changed your life, but
exchanged it forever. If you are not clear on this truth,
we will address it more in the next chapter. But in the
meantime, we want to begin to grab hold of the gift
of grace. No matter how deep, how wide, how high,
or how far your sin goes, His love and grace go further
still! Can you fathom it? He loves you, and if you are
in Jesus, you have been given the free gift of grace!
What do we have to do to receive this lavish gift? "For
by grace you have been saved through faith; and that
not of yourselves, it is the gift of God" (Ephesians 2:8).
Thus, if you are a believer in Christ, grace is a gift, and
it is yours to open and receive! So let me ask you, child
of God, do you realize the gift you have been given
through Christ?

I have a friend who, as a child, bought a prized Christmas gift for his father. He had spent weeks seeking out odd jobs in order to save up enough money to buy the present he had in mind. He wanted nothing more than to please his father and show him his deep admiration for him. One Saturday afternoon the boy traveled by bus downtown to the store that carried the desired item. He bought it and returned home, eagerly anticipating his father's face upon receiving the gift he had worked so hard to give. On Christmas morning he anxiously waited while his father went through his pile of presents. Finally, his father picked up the gift that held value way beyond its price tag. The paper was opened, as if in slow motion, with the son's eyes glued on his father's face. The young boy waited with expectation of his father's expression of gratitude. There was none. The father looked casually at the gift, laid it aside, and went on to the next box wrapped with pretty paper. The valued gift that was given with such anticipation and retrieved at such a high cost, was casually placed aside, its intimate worth unrecognized.

As we walk out our lives in Christ, the gift of grace can be unintentionally neglected in a similar way. Perhaps when you received Christ you thanked Him for the gift of grace in your life, but how much have you consciously utilized it? How much have you allowed yourself to bask in it, to get familiar with it, or appreciate the priceless value of it?

As I rub shoulders with believers in the church of

God, I have come to realize that many of us don't really understand the gift of grace. Overall, few of us seem to have little more than an intellectual knowledge of what the grace of second chances actually offers. Many of us have heard sermons about it. We've let the word *grace* roll off our tongue more times than we can count. We consistently thank God for it. But, for the most part, grace in our daily lives has been consistently misunderstood or unconsciously unapplied. That is largely what this book is about: a second chance to *receive* the gift of grace, *believe* that it's for you, and then *rest* in the identity grace offers the people of God *in* Christ Jesus.

Grace is a powerful truth, wrapped up in the blood of Christ, with your very name on the gift tag. It is a precious and costly present that is given to each and every believer. Jesus paid for it Himself, and it is His desire that we receive it and open it up with the fervency it deserves.

GRACE: God's Radical Acceptance Covenantly Entwined

The Greek word for "grace" in the New Testament is *charis*, which means "acceptable, unearned or unmerited favor."[1] This acronym—**G**od's **R**adical

---

1. Spiros Zodiates, *The Complete Word Study New Testament* (Chattanooga, TN: AMG Publishers, 1992), Lexical Aids to the New Testament.

Acceptance **C**onvenantly **E**ntwined—will help us remember the meaning of grace practically and help us begin to apply it to our lives. We want to meditate on the truth until it makes its way into the depth of our minds and hearts.

First, in Christ, we are radically and completely accepted by God. Second, the power of His grace is supernaturally woven into our identity as believers: covenantly entwined! We will look at that truth more in-depth in the next chapter. In the meantime, recognize the truth that grace is the channel through which all that Christ has for us flows. "Unmerited favor" is a common definition, but it is *through that favor* that God's radical acceptance paves the way for His forgiveness, His righteousness, His power, and His presence in our daily lives. The abundance of grace that He lavishes on us reveals that He not only loves us—He likes us! Grace through Christ makes us incomprehensibly His!

When my boys were little I would tuck them in bed, and we would laugh, cuddle, and converse about whatever was on our minds. I would often end our time by asking them a series of "Do I love you because. . . ?" questions: "Do I love you because you always obey me?" "Do I love you because you picked up your toys?" "Do I love you because your ears are in the right place?" "Do I love you because you're handsome?" They would smile, giggle, and shake their heads back and forth in response to each question. The last question was always the same, "Then why do I love you?" And they would look up at me with their big, naive, laughing eyes, and we would whisper the answer together— "Because you're mine!"

Your Father loves you. . .just because you're His! As you open the gift of grace, will you open your eyes to the truth that God's grace is not dependent upon how good you are, how hard you try, or how much you do for Him? In Christ, we are granted the gift of grace every day, no matter what! God wants you to understand that *in* Christ, you will never be more righteous than you are right now. His grace is forever exceeding, increasing, and more abundant than any sin you have ever committed or will ever commit. Grace invites us to stop trying and start trusting. He is longing to wrap you up in His acceptance and kindness— through grace—every day! To many of us, God is granting a do-over, right here, right now. Will we take Him up on it?

What Grace Is Not

Grace is *not* mercy. Mercy is *not* giving us what we *do* deserve. In other words, before we knew Christ, we deserved hell, but God gave us mercy. The compassion of God is shown in His mercy toward us. Grace is giving us what we *don't* deserve. We don't deserve heaven, or forgiveness of sins, or eternal life. But in His grace,

He gives us those good things anyway. Grace gives us divine, exhilarating, eternal, abundant life in Christ!

Grace is *not* dependant on our holiness. No matter how we perform, no matter how many poor choices we make, grace remains in place through the atonement of Jesus Christ. We can never *do* more to secure God's favor in our lives. Grace is offered unconditionally. So where does holiness fit in? After all, God says we are to be holy because He is holy (see 1 Peter 1:16) and to discipline or train ourselves "for the purpose of godliness" (1 Timothy 4:7).

Robert Allen of Living from His Life International describes New Testament commands as "acceptance-based-performance commands—not performance-based-acceptance commands." We obey God because we are *already* accepted, not in order to *earn* acceptance. Christ has made us acceptable to God already! A life of holiness is our response to God. The Word says that the love of God compels us (see 2 Corinthians 5:14 NKJV) and that we love Him "because He first loved us" (1 John 4:19). As we receive God's perfect love, the desire to live holy lives is a natural overflow of His love compelling us to do so. We live holy lives because we want to, not because we have to.

As believers, we are called to "walk" in both grace (a part of who we *are*) and holiness (a part of what we *do*). What does that look like? Although it's a weak analogy, I like to think of it this way. All of us have a dominant leg—the stronger of the two lower limbs and the one we use to catch ourselves when we start to fall or lose our balance. Grace is our "dominant" leg, our stabilizing power. Without grace, we are not going anywhere. Grace keeps us from falling; grace catches us when we trip; grace goes before us. There can be no step of holiness without the initial step of grace. Grace steps forward and makes a way. Holiness follows. Both move us onward and make us effective in our walk. But holiness doesn't get us to heaven—grace does!

Grace is God's abundant response to us. Holiness is our response to God. Although grace can stand alone, our Christian walk will fall apart when we try to stand on holiness alone. Holiness by itself becomes performance-based religion. (We will discuss that more in a later chapter.) Without grace we wouldn't have a leg to stand on!

Many of us don't *feel* holy and therefore find it difficult to receive grace. One woman I spoke with recently confessed, "I just don't feel like I'm good enough for God to love me. So I find myself living at a distance from Him because I feel afraid to get close." Another friend had shared that she feels constantly ashamed and that she'll never measure up no matter how much she tries to follow God.

Beloved, God is giving us a do-over to see ourselves the way He sees us. At one point in time we were unlovable. We were full of sin and children of wrath. But if you have been made new in Christ—you have a new identity. You may *feel* unlovable, unworthy, or

ashamed, but God *sees* you as priceless. The God of the universe allowed His Son to be killed so that we could be given new life *in* Him. Who are we to give it up so easily? We have been given a second chance to open our eyes to the vastness of all Christ has given us through grace!

About nine years ago our family moved from a house in town to the country. We had wanted a little more room for our three active boys to be able to play outside. Beyond our backyard is a large empty field lined with trees along the horizon. Smack in the middle of the field is a lone oak tree that stands with its branches stretched out against the sky. Wherever we go in the back of the house, there's the view of that magnificent oak tree, showing off its size and strength.

One evening at dinner the oak was the topic of conversation. One of our boys, longing for adventure, asked if we might possibly make our way back through the field someday soon to see the massive tree.

A few days later, the troops were rallied and we set out. Although the oak looked large from our house, the closer we got, the more we realized we had underestimated its size. When we finally arrived, the boys and I were mesmerized by how vast and grand this oak tree actually was. We all stood at the bottom of the large trunk, looking up into the strength of its limbs. The branches over our heads were as large as most tree trunks found on the ground. After a few minutes of attempting to digest its size, one of the boys tried to get his arms around the massive base. It was unachievable. What God had put together, man could never grasp.

I haven't made it out yet to the great redwoods in California, but that oak tree gave me a small sense of what they must be like. To stand in the midst of something so huge, so vast, so steadfast, and strong was captivating. It just awed us. That's just a little bit of how I feel about the vastness of God's grace. From a distance this grace looks doable, acceptable, even comfortable. It tends to blend in with all the other attributes of Christianity. It's just grace, after all. But up close. . .it's measureless! It is more immense, more established, and more awe-inspiring. It's something we will never be able to get our arms around. God's grace in our lives will not be moved! Whether we want to receive it or not—Christ chose to give it to us anyway, lavishly! Beloved, we have a personal invitation to get up close and personal with the grace of second chances. Won't you join me?

The Lord invites us to come close, sit at His feet, and look up into the face of grace. For those of you who feel far away from God, please accept the invitation He offers you. In the book of Luke, Jesus has an encounter with two women He deeply loved. Many of you are familiar with the story of Mary and Martha. Read the following account from Luke 10:38–42:

Now as they were traveling along, He entered a village; and a woman named Martha welcomed Him into her home. She had a sister called Mary, who was seated at the Lord's feet, listening to His word. But Martha was distracted with all her preparations; and she came up to Him and said, "Lord, do You not care that my sister has left me to do all the serving alone? Then tell her to help me." But the Lord answered and said to her, "Martha, Martha, you are worried and bothered about so many things; but only one thing is necessary, for Mary has chosen the good part, which shall not be taken away from her."

First of all, notice two things: where Mary is and what she is doing—sitting at Jesus' feet, listening to His word. Now I want you to picture Mary sitting there, looking up into His face, and listening intently to everything that He was sharing with her. We don't know for sure what Jesus was telling her, but we do know it was much more than our first impressions would imagine. Let me explain. In the New Testament there are two words in the Greek language for "word": *logos* and *rhema*. The word *logos* is defined as "the expression of thought. . .the revealed will of God. . .the sum of God's utterances."[2] This word *logos* is more clearly understood when contrasted with the other Greek word

2   W.E. Vine, *Vine's Expository Dictionary of Old and New Testament Words* (Nashville, TN: Thomas Nelson, Inc., 1997), 1241–1242.

used in the New Testament, *rhema*, which means: "that which is spoken, what is uttered in speech or writing, of a statement, command, instruction."[3]

Rhema is more commonly used to refer to the specific commands and instructions of God: "I can do all things through Him [Christ] who strengthens me" (Philippians 4:13) or "Greater is He who is in you than he who is in the world" (1 John 4:4). The word as *logos* has a much broader meaning that includes the concepts, reasoning, and depth of expressions depicted in the Word of God. One leaf of the magnificent oak spoken of earlier could be used as an example of rhema, whereas the entire oak would be representative of logos. Logos is the sum or whole; rhema is a specific part of the whole.

The word *logos* is the one we want to grasp in this particular passage in Luke. Although *logos* is used often throughout the New Testament, there are two places where it might be more profoundly understood. The first place is in John 1:1, "In the beginning was the *Word*, and the *Word* was with God, and the *Word* was God" (emphasis added). The second place is in Revelation 19:11–13 (emphasis added):

And I saw heaven opened, and behold, a white horse, and He who sat on it is called Faithful and True, and in righteousness He judges and wages war. His eyes are a flame of fire, and on His head are many diadems; and He

---

3. Ibid., 1242.

has a name written on Him which no one knows except Himself. He is clothed with a robe dipped in blood, and His name is called The Word of God.

The Word is the *logos* in each of these examples, the sum of God's utterances, the concept and expression of God, embodied in the Christ, the chosen One, Jesus.

In Luke 10:38–42, the author paints a very intimate picture of Jesus and Mary. Mary is sitting at the feet of Jesus, staring into the face of the *Logos* of God. She is not simply sitting at His feet, listening to specific commands or instruction (rhema). She is sitting at His feet, absorbing "the sum of God's utterances." She is not only absorbed in what He is saying but in the "whole of God" in Jesus. She is focused on every expression, drawn into the depth of *all* that He is, looking deeply into His eyes to see the truth, the person, the God that lies behind them. She is drinking in the living Word, immersed in His presence. She is staring into all that is life, peace, joy, and satisfaction. She has put herself in position to commune with the Face of Grace. She sits before the promised Christ of the Old Testament and the revealed Christ of the New Testament. "The Alpha and the Omega. . .who is and who was and who is to come, the Almighty" (Revelation 1:8). Mary is sitting at the feet of the *Logos* of God.

This, beloved, is the very place Jesus is calling us to sit. As we continue to unpack the vast truth and power of the grace of second chances, we are invited to take the position that Mary did. We are receiving a divine summons to sit at His feet, to stare into the depth of all that He is, and open our hearts wide and unsuspecting. Trust Him. If you haven't already, you have been invited to an intimate do-over. Wrap yourself up in the gift of grace!

1. Have you neglected the gift of grace in your Christian life?

2. In Ephesians 2:8 Paul says grace is "*not of yourselves, it is the gift of God*" (emphasis added). Why do you suppose those three words are included in the verse?

3. Why do we so easily give up the grace of God in our daily lives? What do you think it means to receive, believe, and rest in the gift of grace?

4. Can you relate to the woman who did not feel worthy enough to be loved by God?

5. In Christ you are forgiven according "to the riches of His grace which He lavished on us" (Ephesians 1:7–8). What do the words riches and lavish imply regarding God's gift of grace in your life?

6. Do you often find yourself tripping over holiness as you try to walk in grace?

7. Are you familiar with the picture of the "Face of Grace" that the author paints through the story of Mary? Are you in the habit of living your life from that position of intimacy? If not, how could you begin?

8. When you look into the face of grace, what do you see? How would you describe the Logos of God?

9. Make it a point to pray consistently for a deeper revelation of God's love and grace in your day-to-day life for the next forty days. Afterward, ask yourself if doing so made a difference in your life. Did it pull you closer to God and others?

Notes:

Notes:

Notes:

Notes:

Notes:

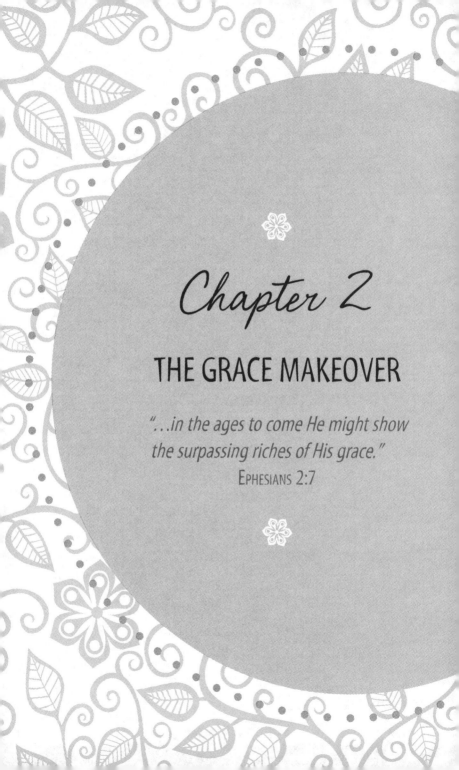

Chapter 2

THE GRACE MAKEOVER

"...in the ages to come He might show the surpassing riches of His grace."
Ephesians 2:7

Once a week for several years, our family would huddle up on the couch, grab some popcorn and blankets, and turn on the television. We were faithful viewers of a show where a team of rescuers would come in, interview a family that needed help, and then build those folks a totally new house. Week after week the viewers were exposed to the heartache of the families, tragedies that had occurred in their lives, or the poor condition of the home that they had lived in due to lack of resources for one reason or another. The family would be sent away for a time and then the renovations team would get to work. Every week the family's original dwelling would be completely destroyed. Within days there would be a brand-new foundation, frame, and roof. A few more days and they were painting rooms beautiful colors and adding wood trim and crystal fixtures. By the time the family members returned, the dwelling they had lived in had had a complete makeover. What was once dull and dilapidated was gone. In its place was a brand-new home. The team would go way above what the viewers would expect, generating oohs and ahs from my crew cuddled on the couch. Sometimes we would look at each other and smile as tears were shed, rejoicing with the celebration going on behind the screen. A brand-new makeover, done in selflessness, would change the family's life as they knew it.

That's what Jesus has done for us on the cross, but in a much more powerful and profound way. This miraculous makeover, offered in selflessness, can change our lives as we know it! Even when we were still dead and dirty in our sin, even before we knew Him, Jesus died on the cross on our behalf. Let's take a fresh look at the gospel and see just how profoundly we have been made over.

First, Jesus paid for our sin. The Bible says, "For the *wages of sin* is death, but the free gift of God is eternal life in Christ Jesus our Lord" (Romans 6:23, emphasis added). His death was the cost required to pay for our sin. Because of His grace, we have been cleansed from *all* sin—yesterday's, today's, and tomorrow's, for all eternity! His blood not only cleanses the conscious sin in our lives, but it goes much deeper. The blood of Jesus reaches to the depths of us, even the hidden places that we cannot see or understand. Join me on an imaginary journey as we take the truth of the gospel and attempt to make it more of a reality in our lives.

I had heard this was the place for spiritual makeovers and that Jesus was the one I needed to see. I had had enough of doing life my way. I had walked in the filth of the world and lived in the wicked pleasures of my own heart. I was done. I knew that no matter what I did, I could never do it on my own. I would never be good enough, smart enough, or pretty enough. To put it simply, I would never be enough. I needed a Savior. Jesus spotted me from across the room. He walked toward me and, extending His hand, invited me over to sit down in the spiritual beauty chair. I came to Him, dead in my sin, smelly, dirty, and rotten to the core. My hair was tangled with mats, and I was helpless, exposed, and ashamed. The stench of my sin filled the room. I told Him I needed Him. I wanted Him to save me. He knew long ago I would come to Him. As He reached out His nail-pierced hand, I reached out to receive what I had been looking for since the very beginning. And with that one touch, I was His. He took His blood and began to wash away my life of sin. His blood cleansed and purified me to the depths. I stared in the mirror. I looked completely different. The smell was gone. The darkness lifted as the light filled the empty space. I glanced behind me in the mirror, and I saw the Face of Grace. He smiled warmly. My eyes filled with tears. Why would Jesus have done that for me?

Christ washed me of my sin, but Christ also became sin *for* me. He didn't just hang there so that we had something to talk about in Sunday school. He actually died in my place. I had gone to church most of my life before I began to grasp the power found in this truth. When Christ hung on the cross, dying, He actually bore our sins on His body (see 1 Peter 2:24). Part of the miraculous makeover of the gospel involves my "old man" dying with Him: "Our old self was crucified *with* Him, in order that our body of sin might be done away with, so that we would no longer be slaves to sin; *for he who has died is freed from sin*" (Romans 6:6–7, emphasis added; see also Galatians 2:20).

Jesus then lifted His arm up above my head, and I watched in the mirror as He re-created a picture of that day two thousand years ago at Golgotha. The scene unfolded before me, and I could hear the stillness of the few people gathered around. It was as if Jesus and I were invisible to the small crowd that surrounded us. Someone was weeping beside me. The sky was dark and the ground was barren. I smelled the stagnant air as my eyes rose to see the body of my beloved Savior on the cross. A perfect, blameless God-man offering His life for mine. I glanced behind me at the Jesus standing with me before the mirror. His eyes met mine as He waited to see if I would understand. I looked back at the scene He had painted before me, my heart captivated by the pain and agony displayed on my Savior's face as He struggled for each breath. The Jesus behind me took the filth, the grime, and the putrid pile of stench that lay on the floor beside me and gently placed it into the vision and upon the One on the cross. The Savior hung in the silence, covered, my black, filthy, putrid sin absorbing into His blood-soaked body. I heard a whisper in my heart. . . . " 'Behold, the Lamb of God who takes away the sin of the world!' "
(John 1:29).

Jesus came around in front of the salon chair so I could see into His face. With His eyes fixed on mine, He reached in and removed my heart of stone. Then He reached into the core of my being and pulled out something dark and rancid. I hadn't even known it was there. He turned to the One on the cross and placed the dark form upon my Savior. It was shaped like me. It looked like me. All of a sudden I knew, that dark part of me that had been born into sin, that craved it, that marked me as Adam's child, was being put to death with Christ. It was the old me. And I was suddenly struck by how ugly it was. I stared in disbelief as I saw Christ in agony with my "death" all over Him. He was so faithful, so loving. He had the power and the ability to come down from the cross. He could have thrown it all off. But He didn't. He just hung there and became sin for me. He lifted His head and His eyes looked directly into mine. They were overflowing with love. He had every reason to hate, to blame, to judge. There was none of that. Only warmth. . .only love. . .only tenderness. As I took it in, I looked behind me in the mirror. "I'm so sorry, Jesus. All this time, and I never really understood." He looked at me with kind and gracious eyes, "Behold, I make all things new."

As sinners, we carried Adam's seed and had an "old" nature that was born into sin, designed to sin, and craved a lifestyle of sin. That was its DNA; that old nature can't do anything else. Upon salvation, Christ ushered us into His death and the "old" nature was crucified with Him. To make a way for the new, God first took care of the "old." In the crucifixion, Christ paid for our sin and crucified the dead "old" man.

But that's just the first half of the gospel. There's more. Our makeover is not yet complete. On the cross Jesus took care of our sins, but we were still empty. What Christ did for us in the resurrection is the second part of the Gospel. When we were saved through faith in Jesus Christ, we were born again—born of the Spirit and given God's DNA. Like Jesus, who was born of the Holy Spirit, we are now God's children and carry the seed of the Holy Spirit of God through our spiritual re-birth. Ephesians 2:4–8 tells us that when Christ rose from the dead, we rose up with Him, and were made *alive in Christ*! The Word adds that "if anyone is in Christ, he is a new creation; old things have passed away; behold, all things have become new" (2 Corinthians 5:17 NKJV). He gave us a new birth and then filled us with His Spirit.

When God our Savior revealed his kindness and love, he saved us, not because of the righteous things we had done, but because of his mercy. He washed away our sins, giving us a new birth and new life through the Holy Spirit. He generously poured out the Spirit upon us through Jesus Christ our Savior. Because of his grace he declared us righteous and gave us confidence that we will inherit eternal life.

TITUS 3:4–7 NLT

He didn't just cleanse us and then send us on our way to try to figure out this Christian life on our own. Jesus made us new, filled us with His spirit, and declared us—*alive in Christ!* "For as in Adam all die, so also in Christ all will be made alive" (1 Corinthians 15:22). Why? So that He might show us the "surpassing riches of His grace" (Ephesians 2:7).

Jesus spun the salon chair around to face Him, turning my back on the image I had been entranced in. He spoke gently, "Child, you are clean, but you are empty. You have been united with Me in death. Are you ready to be united with Me in life?" After all that, Christ wasn't finished. The cleaned vessel needed to be filled. I nodded my head, trusting, knowing that in my humanness I would only receive by faith the makeover awaiting me. Through the kindness of His grace He reached inside me and placed a heart of flesh where the heart of stone had been (see Ezekiel 36:26). He took His pure divine nature and placed it in the core of my being, where the dark old nature had been. He looked into my eyes and smiled. "I have known you from the beginning. You are My covenant child. I delight in you. You are deeply loved, fully forgiven, radically accepted, completely pleasing, and made complete in Me." In case there was any doubt of my new identity, Jesus bent over me and breathed the living Holy Spirit into my inner being, sealing all that had been made new. I was a new creation. What was lost had now been found; what was dead had been made alive. The surpassing riches of

His grace manifested in me by my new life in Christ. The gospel of God! Then with a big smile He spun me around so that I could see myself in the mirror. I couldn't help but smile in response, and we both let out a hearty laugh. This was the One that I would live in, laugh with, serve, and enjoy the rest of my eternal life. And with that, He pulled a beautiful robe from behind Him and wrapped me in His righteousness. "You have been made new, beloved. I have wrapped you up in all that I AM and I give you My life to live. Don't forget who you are." And the Father's words echoed in my heart, "Christ in you, the hope of glory" (Colossians 1:27).

Why would God do all that for us? Do you find yourself staring up into the oak tree, trying to get your arms around just how "surpassingly rich" and lavish His grace is? Jesus gave us the makeover of all makeovers. He cleaned up our mess of sin with the beauty of Himself. He took our dead "old man," crucified it with Himself, and then gave us His life to live instead! When He rose from the dead, we rose with Him. Each of us is a *new* creation. Beloved, if you have never looked into the Face of Grace to this extent, now is the time. "I have been crucified with Christ; and it is no longer I who live, but Christ lives in me; and the life which I now live in the flesh I live by faith in the Son of God, who loved me and gave Himself up for me" (Galatians 2:20). Did you catch that? If not, go back and read that verse again slowly, out loud. We are to *receive, believe,* and *rest in* the truth that Jesus gave us His life! On the cross, God performed "the great exchange." Jesus took our dead, empty lives and "exchanged" them with His. Look how Martin Luther describes it:

> Learn Christ and him crucified. Learn to sing to him and, despairing of yourself, say, "Lord Jesus, you are my righteousness, just as I am your sin. You have taken upon yourself what is mine and have given me what is yours. You have taken upon yourself what you were not and have given to me what I was not.

When I first sat down in that spiritual beauty chair, I knew I needed cleansing. What I didn't realize is how much I needed His life *in* me. The life I now live is Christ's life. It is not mine anymore. He crucified my old nature and replaced it with His divine nature (see 2 Peter 1:4). Christ gave me His life! *New* life *in* Christ! He gave me Himself (see Galatians 2:20)! He gave me His righteousness (see Romans 5:19)! He gave me His inheritance (see 1 Peter 1:4)! He gave me His reward! He gave me His home (see John 14:3)! He gave me His peace (see John 14:27)! He gave me His mind (see 1 Corinthians 2:16)! He gave me His power (see Ephesians 3:16)! He gave me His Father! He gave me His Spirit (see 2 Corinthians 1:22)! He gave me all that He could aside from making me God. And we all know He couldn't do that! (We wouldn't want Him to!) So He did the next best thing. . .He made me His child (see John 1:12)! He has given us everything (see 2 Peter 1:3)! In His grace, He has held nothing back! Why? Because He loves us! And it's all wrapped up in the free, lavish gift of grace through Jesus, the Christ! Do you see the face of grace? Do you see the vastness of the gift?

Oh child of God, we have yet to understand how much power lies in the gospel of Jesus Christ. But the God of second chances wants us to give it a try. So wrap yourself up in His grace and move forward, knowing that He loves you and that He gave Himself up in order for you to live in Him and all that He is. Not just life *in* eternity, but *for* eternity—and it starts right now. You don't have to wait till you get to heaven. He wants you to know Him and what He has freely given you so that you may have life in Him, every day, now and forever. Not a casual, complacent life, but an abundant, purposeful life, dependent upon His Spirit and His righteousness living *through* you and *in* you.

Not only does your identity involve Christ living *in* you, but the Bible also says that you are *in* Christ. He is *in* you and you are *in* Him. As we have already established, "if anyone is *in* Christ, he is a new creature" (2 Corinthians 5:17, emphasis added). "Even so consider yourselves to be dead to sin, but alive to God *in* Christ Jesus" (Romans 6:11, emphasis added). "The free gift of God is eternal life *in* Christ Jesus our Lord" (Romans 6:23, emphasis added). The phrases "in Christ," "in Him," and "in the Lord," appear 164 times throughout Paul's letters. In the Word of God, *in* is a word we probably read over again and again without realizing its powerful significance. In the Greek, the little word *in* in this context means: "in a fixed position,"[4] "with a primary idea of rest in any place or thing," remaining in, surrounded in, enveloped in.[5] Let me sum it up for you. *In Christ you are: fixed in. . .resting in. . .remaining in. . .surrounded in. . .enveloped in. . .HIM!* Not only does Jesus want you to believe that He is in you and wants to live His life through you, but He also wants you to believe that you are *in* Him. He wants our identity to be found *in* Him, not in us, our own abilities, our family, what we do, our good behavior, or our moral religion.

As children of God, the little word *in* takes us to an amazing place. Let's stop and think about where *in* can take you. Imagine. . .*in* the ocean. . .*in* the sky. . . *in* space. . .*in* trouble. . .*in* love. . .*in* the mall (sorry, couldn't resist). . . . The seemingly insignificant *in* takes us to a place where we are completely encompassed. Beloved, because you are fixed *in*, resting *in*, remaining *in*, surrounded *in*, and enveloped *in* Christ, you know He's got you covered—inside and out.

---

4. Spiros Zodiates, *The Complete Word Study New Testament* (Chattanooga, TN: AMG Publishers, 1992), Greek Dictionary of the New Testament.
5. Ibid., Lexical Aids to the New Testament.

GRACE: God's Radical Acceptance Covenantly Entwined

Do you see how radically acceptable you are because you are His covenant child? You now have the Spirit of Christ living in you. You are a child of the Father and you have His DNA. Inside and out, God's lavish grace is manifested in you through Jesus Christ. Grace is not something that accompanies us; it is His "makeover" supernaturally created in us. Just like the circulatory system spreads and delivers life throughout our body—so the grace of God is interwoven in us as *new* creatures. If we were to dissect our new nature in a "supernatural" science lab, we would find a miraculous circulatory system of grace woven into the fibers of our being. This system constantly washes every "spiritual" cell in our body. We could never walk away from it, cut it out, or scrub it off. Can you picture yourself trying to walk away from or dissecting yourself of all of your blood vessels, capillaries, or veins? Our very life source would be stripped away. We would not be able to exist. It is the same with our identity *in* Christ. The grace of God is forever delivering His miraculous acceptance, even to the deepest, darkest depths within us. There is no getting away from grace through Christ. No getting out from under the favor of God. Can you see the woman in the beauty chair trying to "undo" what Christ did? There is no part of us that is not touched or transformed by this work of grace. It is divine. It is unified in us. It is our identity.

If this is who God says I am, then how come I don't *feel* like that's who I am? God's Word is truth. It is alive and active. Though our feelings are important and God-given, we have to remember that they are not always correct indicators of truth. Whether we choose to believe it or not, God made us, sees us, and treats us as new creations in Christ. In order to "experience" His grace, we need to begin to see ourselves in the same way.

In *Classic Christianity*, Bob George says that if some-one saw a butterfly he or she would never refer to it as a colorful converted worm. One would no longer think of this new creature as what it once was (a worm) because it would be seen for what it is now—a beautiful butterfly.

God sees us the same way. We are new in Christ. We might not always act like a new creature. The butterfly might go hang out with his worm chums or do things that good butterflies shouldn't, but it will never be a worm again. It will always be a butterfly! [6]

We have had a spiritual makeover. In Christ we are new creatures, entwined with grace, and invited to live each day from a position of intimate unity *in* Him. Although this doesn't mean that we will never sin, it does mean that we no longer have the same nature that craves sin. Our new nature wants what God wants. When we begin to walk in the truth of who we really are *in* Christ, we begin to understand how foolish it is to resort

6. Bob George, *Classic Christianity* (Eugene, OR: Harvest House Publishers, 1989), 73–74.

back to the way we were. To choose sin contradicts our new nature. Why would perfect and blameless "butterflies" that are now made in the image of Christ, clothed *in* Christ, and filled with the Spirit of Christ, live like they're worms? The more clearly we understand our identity, the more we desire to live it out.

In the book *Grace Walk*, Steve McVey describes his continuous struggle with feelings of condemnation as a Christian until he began to understand his new identity. The Bible says we are no longer condemned when we are in Christ. All of God's condemnation against sin was put upon Jesus as He hung on the cross. McVey communicates that when he sins now the Holy Spirit reminds him of his new identity in Christ, and he sees the foolishness of choosing sin. Remembering his God-given identity, he senses a desire to leave sin behind and move forward as a fully forgiven, radically accepted saint in Christ.[7]

In order for us to be able to live this truth out practically every day, we need to believe God's Word. We need to put into practice what we know is true. We meditate on the "seed" of God's Word until it "sows" its way into our hearts and minds. In the book of James, the author writes, "In humility receive the word implanted, which is able to save your souls. But prove yourselves doers of the word. . . . One who looks intently at the perfect law, the law of liberty, and abides by it, not having become a forgetful hearer but an

7.   Steve McVey, *Grace Walk* (Eugene, OR: Harvest House Publishers, 1995), 51.

effectual doer, this man will be blessed in what he does" (James 1:21–22, 25). Much too often, we tuck away the truth of God in a "spiritual" pocket to save for later. But these verses tell us to receive what the Word says and abide by it. *Abide* means to make a home with it. Not forget about it, place it aside, or just think of it now and then. We need to *believe*, *receive*, and *rest in* the truth day in and day out until it becomes "home" to us, thus "implanting" the seed of the living Word within us in such a way that it will take root and bear fruit. We have been made new *in* Christ, whether we feel like it or not. To bring this truth "home," focus and meditate on who you are *in* Christ.

I love James Robison's analogy of the bird dog. A good bird dog is well-trained, focused, and knows exactly what he is hunting for. But an untrained bird dog will chase everything that crosses its path. Every little chipmunk, squirrel, or moth that comes up out of the grass would be a constant distraction. But if a good bird dog is looking for quail, that bird dog will keep his eyes and his nose peeled for one thing and one thing only— quail. [8] When we are focused on sowing the truth of God into our lives, we need to act like a good bird dog.

As you go about your day, no matter what comes across your path, allow God to train you up to know "one" thing: you *in* Christ, and Christ *in* you. In Christ, you are a new creation. That is your true identity. Sit back down in the beauty chair and take a good look in

8. James Robison, *Racing Jesus* (Fort Worth, TX: LIFE Publishing, 2009), 90–91.

the "spiritual" mirror. Christ smiles at you even now—beholding the beauty He died for you to have. You have been made over, beloved of God, and it is no longer you who live, but Christ lives in you. Grab hold of the gift of grace!

Discussion Questions

1. Why is understanding our identity in Christ so important?

2. Do you regularly meditate on the cost that Christ paid for you to walk in your new identity in Him? How might dwelling on that truth change your heart?

3. How might realizing and accepting your identity in Christ affect your relationship with Jesus, yourself, and others?

4. What does it mean to believe God? What lies do you dwell on that seem to smother the truth God speaks to you?

5. How often do you let your feelings, rather than the Word of God, dictate who you are? Why is it important to choose to believe God over feelings?

6. What does Ephesians 2:4–8 say about God? What does it say about us?

7. How would you describe the "exchanged" life?

8. Write down Galatians 2:20 on an index card, and place it somewhere you will see it every day. Try to memorize it as you meditate on it day after day. Ask God for continued revelation as to what this truth means in your daily life.

9. What bird-dog truth from this chapter do you want to apply to your daily life?

Notes:

Notes:

Notes:

Notes:

Notes:

....

....

....

....

....

....

....

....

....

....

....

....

....

....

....

....

....

....

....

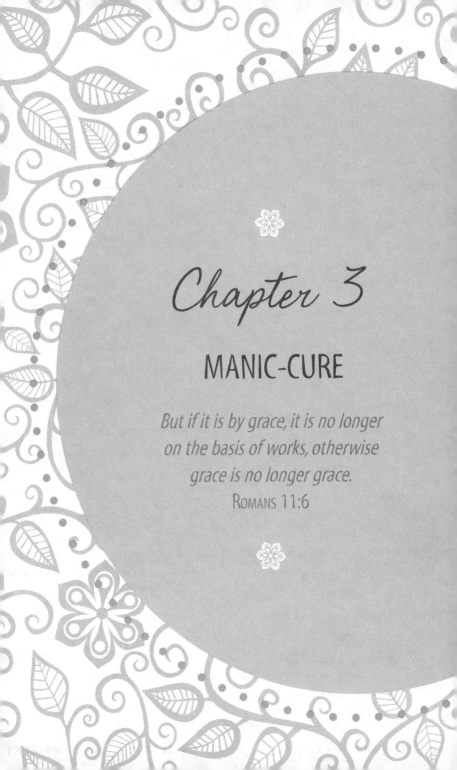

Chapter 3

MANIC-CURE

*But if it is by grace, it is no longer
on the basis of works, otherwise
grace is no longer grace.*
ROMANS 11:6

A friend of mine was getting married in a few months. One afternoon she called me with a spontaneous request to accompany her to the local mall. She was planning a quick shopping spree for "honeymoon" attire and wanted a second opinion, so I cleared my schedule. When we arrived at the store we immediately began scanning the racks for potential outfits that might be appropriate for the occasion. Within a short time we had both contributed to the cart, piling up a playful but romantic "leaning tower of pleez-im" for her time away.

We pushed the loaded cart to the changing room and made our way in. Upon her insistence, I joined her in the small booth behind the curtain in order to be available for any warranted opinions she solicited. The space was somewhat limited, but it echoed with the laughter of two good friends as we began making our way through the pile. The game was on, and it was one outfit after another, followed by varying comments and observations. Slow and steady, piece by piece, between laughter and elbows, we became completely engulfed in the celebration of it all. Her face glowed, and she smiled from ear to ear as she shared the latest wedding details and her excitement about the trip. I continued to replace clothing back on hangers and give my opinions when necessary. Then it happened. I had turned my eyes away, more out of respect than necessity, as she tried on a somewhat "scant" article of clothing. Next thing I knew she was calling out to me with muffled cries of desperation mixed with laughter. I turned to see my friend completely bound in a thin, see-through negligee stuck over her head, with one arm pinned down by her side and the other sticking straight out the top of the neckline. Her pretty face, distorted by the tight veil of material stretched tightly across it, was half laughing, half begging for release from this "second skin." Pork sausage in casing came to mind. Yes, it was that tight! The laughter spilled out of both of us as I tried to grab hold of any piece of accessible garment, wanting desperately to help my friend, though not wanting to make the situation any more painful. I'm not sure how long the struggle continued, however, I am quite sure that we were the main event in the changing room that day.

My friend and I battled with that particular garment until the piece of restricted clothing was removed, and she was able to put on something that was much more complimentary. We might have been somewhat breathless from laughter, but overall we both came out unscathed. In the Christian walk, however, that is not always the case. Often as believers, we are "bound" by things we were never meant to wear.

No matter how you wear it, putting on anything other than the pure gospel of Jesus will bind us every time. As Christians, one of our greatest temptations is to add to what Jesus accomplished on the cross. We buy into the lie that it still depends on us. We put on rule upon rule, expectation piled upon expectation, our own opinions, others' comments, a few Bible verses, and before we know it, "something" doesn't feel right, and we find ourselves confined in a garment that doesn't fit.

God's law is good when used lawfully. "Through the Law comes the knowledge of sin" (Romans 3:20) and makes people "*accountable* to God" (Romans 3:19, emphasis added), but following the law will never make us *acceptable* before God. Galatians 2:16 says, "man is not justified by the works of the Law but through faith in Christ Jesus." In other words, the law was meant to show us our sin. The law is God's tool that *always points us back to the gospel*. The gospel is not *about* Jesus. It *is* Jesus. If we put our faith in the *works* of the law, then grace is no longer grace, and we have traded the pure gospel of Christ, dependent on God, for a counterfeit gospel that depends on man. In other words, we end up following a list of rules in order to try to achieve righteousness rather than accepting the righteousness of Christ. The glorious makeover we received in the spiritual beauty chair is hidden beneath our own self-effort.

Putting on a wardrobe of works disguises the pure gospel of Christ. It places a perpetual emphasis on behavior, which causes our eyes to remain on what we *do* rather than who we *are*. Someone once said: there are two kinds of people in the world; those who are constantly finding fault with themselves and those who are constantly finding fault with someone else. Our obsession with a spiritual inventory of right and wrong catapults us into excessive self-examination. We determine who is acceptable to God depending on what list of rules we follow. The most sincere believers are usually the most susceptible. With each failed attempt to get it right, we grow more restless, feeling frustrated and defeated. We forget who we are and stand in front of the spiritual mirror, modeling a religious wardrobe of our own effort, wisdom, strength, and traditions. Most of us who ride this manic roller coaster are well-meaning people trying to get it right. Even with a genuine desire to please the Father, so many of us are growing weary with knowing how to *do* the Christian life. We can so easily feel like our offering isn't nearly enough. What we fail to realize is. . .it isn't.

Let me ask you this one question: Did you receive the [Holy] Spirit as the result of obeying the Law and doing its works, or was it by hearing [the message of the Gospel] and believing [it]? [Was it from observing a law of rituals or from a message of faith?] Are you so foolish and so senseless and so silly? Having begun [your new life spiritually] with the [Holy] Spirit, are you now reaching perfection [by dependence] on the flesh?

GALATIANS 3:2–3 AMP

The "gospel of works" sends us down a path that sounds Christian, looks Christian, but is void of the pure gospel of Jesus Christ. Beloved, in order to grab hold of the grace of second chances, we need to learn how to recognize it in our own lives. In Max Lucado's book, *In the Grip of Grace,* he shares a detailed description of a subtle garment that is reflective of dressing up in a wardrobe other than the one Christ provides. Lucado describes a dapper suit that he tailored himself. He says the pants were representative of the good works he accomplished, hours of study he put toward his lessons, and projects he completed. Many people flattered him on how good he looked and how well done his works were. He goes on to describe a coat of conviction, symbolic of his passion and religious earnestness, that was worn with the pants. He wore his coat so impressively that he was often invited to speak and model it for others. To top off the pants and coat, he wore his hat of intelligence, woven with his own hands with the "fabric of personal opinion." Lucado concludes that even God must be proud of his suit of skill and proficiency. He describes going before the throne in prayer, expecting God to be blessed by his hard work and many accomplishments for the Kingdom. But God was silent. "Surely, God admires all I am doing," he thought to himself. Little by little his wardrobe began to fray and grow flimsy. So he began to work harder, to plan more, and to strategize differently. But the suit kept unraveling. He tried stitching it back together and patching it here and there, but despite his best efforts, his suit went to ruins. He grew tired from all his failed attempts to keep his suit together and his body warmed. So he returned to God with a vulnerable, weary prayer. "God, I feel naked." God gently and compassionately reassured him he had been naked for quite a while. And then God, in His goodness, picked up a regal robe that would never unravel and wrapped it around his naked body. "Child, you are clothed in Christ."[9]

Christ has clothed us (see Galatians 3:27). He is our wardrobe. When we try to dress ourselves in anything other than Him, we are covering up the simple but profound power of the gospel. Because of our new identity, we are called to live *in* a person, not *by* a list of rules, a polished performance, or people's endless expectations. We come to Christ through faith because we realize that on our own, no matter how hard we strive, we will never achieve the righteousness of God. God knew that, too, and that's why He sent Christ to die for us. And it is too rich a gospel, too powerful a sacrifice, to be replaced with the poor and wretched efforts of man.

Paul says in Galatians 2:21: "I do not nullify the grace of God, for if righteousness comes through the Law, then Christ died needlessly." Paul is saying that trying to *do* it right in order to make us *feel* righteous

---

9. Max Lucado, *In the Grip of Grace* (Dallas: Word, 1996), xi.

nullifies grace! If it's all about doing it right, then Christ didn't need to die! We can unconsciously make the law our God, and *doing* it right, our savior. God has already made our provision. Grace and truth come through Jesus Christ. In Christ, we *are* righteous whether we *feel* like it or not! Christianity isn't sin management; it's a relationship with Jesus Christ. If you insist on fighting, fight to rest *in* Him. Fight to *rest* in grace!

Have you ever seen a dog getting ready to lie down in his bed? It looks as if he's chasing his tail as he goes around and around, nose to tail, tail to nose, time and again, before he's determined the spot is ready for napping. I sometimes think that is the way we must look in our manic Christianity as we chase our own tail of works. If you think it through, a works-based gospel will always keep the focus on self-do, self-do, self-do. Round and round we go chasing our tails, as if it all depends on us. It's no wonder our works-based Christianity makes us feel like we are going in circles. Grab hold of the grace of second chances. Christ alone stops us from spinning and puts us at rest.

The first major symptom of a works-based wardrobe is that, no matter how we *do* it, our *do* will never be enough. Who of us can see straight when we're chasing our tails? As we learn to fix our eyes on Jesus, "the author and perfecter of faith" (Hebrews 12:2), the Holy Spirit will be diligent to remind us what needs to be addressed in our lives in order to glorify Him. We will be well-suited to live a life full of Him: His gospel, His strength, and His righteousness.

Paul challenges the believers in Galatia: why would we try to finish in works what we have already begun in the Holy Spirit (see Galatians 3:3)? In other words, why would we see that we are not "enough," receive Christ as Savior, and then after a while, move out of faith and go back to trying to be "enough?" Silly, isn't it? Silly, but subtle. Remember, beloved, the law was given to point us to the gospel. In the book of Romans, Paul reminds us that being *ruled* by rules is no longer part of our identity in Christ:

> But now we have been released from the law, for we died to it and are no longer captive to its power. Now we can serve God, not in the old way of obeying the letter of the law, but in the new way of living in the Spirit.
>
> ROMANS 7:6 NLT (EMPHASIS ADDED)

> Therefore there is now no condemnation for those who are in Christ Jesus. For the law of the Spirit of life in Christ Jesus has set you free from the law of sin and death.
>
> ROMANS 8:1–2 (EMPHASIS ADDED)

Believers, we are now under the law of the Spirit. The Bible also calls it "the law of Christ" (Galatians 6:2) and "the law of liberty" (James 1:25). This new law actually holds us to a higher standard. The Old Testament says

we should love our neighbor as we love ourselves. But Jesus raised the standard. He said to love others "as I have loved you" (John 13:34). We are no longer to love the way *we* would love. Instead, we are to love the way *Jesus* would love! However, we can't accomplish this standard by following the rules. It will only be accomplished by the Spirit of God in us. The Spirit helps us understand what the Bible *means*, not just what it *says*. It is the Spirit that causes us to know the thoughts of God and discern spiritual truths (see 1 Corinthians 2:11–14). Under the law of the Spirit we "walk by the Spirit" (Galatians 5:16), are "led by the Spirit" (Galatians 5:18), and "live by the Spirit" (Galatians 5:25). The Spirit within us marks us as children of Abba God (see Galatians 4:6), and the power of the Spirit produces within us the character of God (see Galatians 5:22–23). The work of the law will never produce the life of the Spirit. We couldn't have a better identity than the one we have *in* Christ. Why would we put on our own filthy rags when He has so graciously clothed us in Him?

The second symptom of a works-based wardrobe is that it is laced with man's agenda. Christ is *in* you, and He wants to live His life through you. We are to be holy because God is holy (see 1 Peter 1:16). Why? So that "'they may see your good works, and glorify your Father who is in heaven'" (Matthew 5:16). We are not to strive in good works so that others might see how good *we* are. Our good works are to be done *in* the Spirit, producing "holy" behavior as an overflow of Christ *in* us, ultimately pointing to the Father.

When we set our mind on man's agenda, we become a stumbling block to God's agenda working through us. Matthew 16 contains a familiar interchange between Jesus and Peter. Jesus is on His way to Jerusalem, describing to His disciples that He must die and be raised again on the third day. Peter, appalled to hear that Jesus was to die in this way, replies, " 'God forbid it, Lord! This shall never happen to You' " (Matthew 16:22). Jesus responded, " 'Get behind Me, Satan! You are a *stumbling block* to Me; for you are not setting your mind on *God's interests*, but *man's*' " (Matthew 16:23, emphasis added). The scripture doesn't tell us if Satan had spiritually influenced Peter, or if he just somehow resembled Satan by his response. What scripture does reveal is that Peter had his mind on the "things of men" rather than on the "things of God" (Matthew 16:23 NKJV). Peter's reply, which reflected man's agenda rather than God's, not only made him *look* like the enemy but made him a stumbling block to the Lord. If we didn't have Jesus to help us see into Peter's heart, he might possibly look very spiritual to us. It's obvious that Peter didn't want something bad to happen to Jesus. But when Peter's agenda is exposed, we can more clearly see the subtlety of man's interests revealed in his heart.

Another example could be found in the interaction between Satan and Jesus, where the latter was tempted three times by the devil in the wilderness (see Matthew 4:1–11). In the first temptation, a hungry Jesus, having just finished a forty-day fast, was challenged to turn stones into bread. Was it an okay desire to eat? Yes, but Jesus was about the will of the Father. His life was all about God's agenda, not His own. He could have turned the stones to bread and satisfied His hunger—but He would have been bowing to His need, His power, His life. He would have been following "man's agenda," not the Father's. In the second temptation, Satan tells Jesus to throw Himself down from the highest point of the temple. Here, in an effort to add legitimacy to his request, the enemy quotes the Word of God. It sounds spiritual, smells spiritual, but we know it's not—it's coming straight from the mouth of the enemy. Jesus uses the Word of God accurately, according to God's agenda, and the enemy moves on to the third temptation. Satan tells Jesus that if He will bow down and worship him "all the kingdoms of the world and their glory" (Matthew 4:8) will be given to Him. Jesus responds a final time with God's word, also known as the "sword of the Spirit" (Ephesians 6:17), and the devil leaves Him.

Why do I bring up this portion of scripture? To more clearly communicate how subtly we can use the Word of God or appear spiritual when all the while we are wearing the wrong stuff. Temptation can come to us in the same way it came to Peter and Jesus. Jesus saw through the "things of man" in order to be faithful to the "things of God." Like Peter, we can be subtly deceived when we do things that look spiritual, sound spiritual, feel spiritual, but are motivated by the "things of man." We are dressed in self-conscious religion that promotes our own agenda and our own unconscious attempts to appear righteous. It is void of a God-conscious agenda and laced with our own. "'For I have come down from heaven, not to do My own will, but the will of Him who sent Me'" (John 6:38).

Are our good works to show people the Father and the pure gospel of Jesus Christ? Or are we going to church every week in a wardrobe that doesn't fit, in a tainted gospel that is self-conscious and marked by man's agenda? The law, when used lawfully, always brings us back to our dependency upon the true gospel of Jesus Christ. And the true gospel will always be saturated with God's agenda. We must rid ourselves of any garment other than the regal robe of the atonement of Jesus Christ.

In *My Utmost for His Highest*, Oswald Chambers challenges the reader to bring every part of his spiritual life to one center: the atonement of Christ. Is Christ becoming the dominant center of your life, or are you allowing your spiritual life to be eaten away? As Christians, we need to examine what keeps us going, what holds us up, what resource we live from. The "great exerting influence" of your life must always be the atonement of Jesus Christ.[10]

It is resting in the atonement of Christ that will

10. Oswald Chambers, *My Utmost for His Highest* (Grand Rapids, MI: Discovery House Publishers, 1963), June 7.

ultimately bring true joy and fervency to the people of God, bringing an end to manic Christianity. A consistent willingness to rest in what Christ has done will be experienced as we abandon our lives to Jesus. It is better for us to be utterly abandoned to God than it is to be holy. Holiness doesn't lead us to abandonment. Abandonment leads us to holiness. Holiness is important, but living *in* His grace is the "dominant leg." As we look into the Face of Grace and get to know Him, His Spirit will lead us down the path of holy living.

The following is a journal entry from a dear sister, Rachele Kauffmann. It beautifully records the subtle battle that can go on within us as we struggle through trying to *do* the right thing and then ultimately wrap ourselves up in His garment of grace:

A ministry team going to India invited me to go along. I prayed about it for a while and felt that the Lord was telling me to go. Initially, I had a peace about it. But as the trip got closer, I began to feel a bit more anxious. What I had thought was a nine-day trip became extended, the cost increased, and I didn't feel that my gifts were needed. There were a number of other people going who could certainly teach any material better than I could.

I lost all sense of peace and was feeling incredibly anxious and doubtful about whether I should even go. It came to a head one night while I was lying in bed. I told the Lord I didn't want to go. "He doesn't need me. He has other people who can do it better. Who will take care of my children? What if something happens to them or to me?" I laid there and cried, arguing with the Lord and pouring out all of my fears. I talked with my husband, hoping he would tell me not to go. He didn't, so I went back to the Lord. He graciously met me right where I was: in my crying and selfish pleading. The Lord clearly said that He would love me if I went and He would love me if I stayed. He also said the number of my days are the same no matter which I choose. He told me that I didn't have to go, I can stay home, but He would like me to go. With His response, my fear fled and my impure motives changed. I didn't have to go because I should, or because it was the godly thing to do. I could go simply because He asked me to. In that realization was the freedom to say yes with a whole heart. I had the assurance that whatever happened, He had it covered. Any remaining doubt was swept away with one final challenge from the Lord: "If one person was saved from hell and would come into a relationship with Me, would it be worth it?"

"Yes, Lord!"

The grace of second chances is by far the greatest cure for spiritual manics that will ever be found. Let's say "yes" with a whole heart to the garment of grace Christ died for us to wear. The cost of grace was high! Let's not waste it. Intentionally, step-by-step, let's receive, believe, and rest all that God is revealing to us about His great gift of grace. As Corrie ten Boom said, "If His will be your wilt and His way be your way, then all of your insufficiency and inaptitude shall be met by the sufficiency of His grace."

We are found *in* Him, beloved. He has clothed us with His "garments of salvation" and a "robe of righteousness" (Isaiah 61:10). It is *in* Him that "we live and move and have our being" (Acts 17:28 NKJV). Move forward, child of God, in a wardrobe that was designed especially for you. You are dressed to accomplish much in His name. Throw off those binding garments and move forward—forever and abundantly clothed *in* Christ (see Galatians 3:27).

Discussion Questions

1. Can you relate to the concept of manic Christianity? If so, how?

2. If you were to describe your "wardrobe of works" what would it look like? How does it compare with what you have in Christ?

3. Have you ever confused man's agenda with God's agenda? What does that look like in your life as a wife, mom, or child of God?

4. How does following the law keep your eyes on yourself? What particular laws, expectations, or rules have you or others put in place that keep you continually self-focused?

5. How can grace be the cure to the answers you gave in the question above?

6. What if the only piece of clothing you had to wear was a garment of grace? In other words—wear grace or go naked? Could you wear it well? Would it fit comfortably?

7. If we saw ourselves as spiritually naked apart from grace, do you think it would be easier to choose the garment of grace daily? Would we more readily recognize the deception of living in our own works?

8. What bird-dog truth from this chapter can you begin to meditate on today and begin apply to your daily life?

Notes:

Notes:

Notes:

Notes:

Notes:

Notes:

....

....

....

....

....

....

....

....

....

....

....

....

....

....

....

....

....

....

....

....

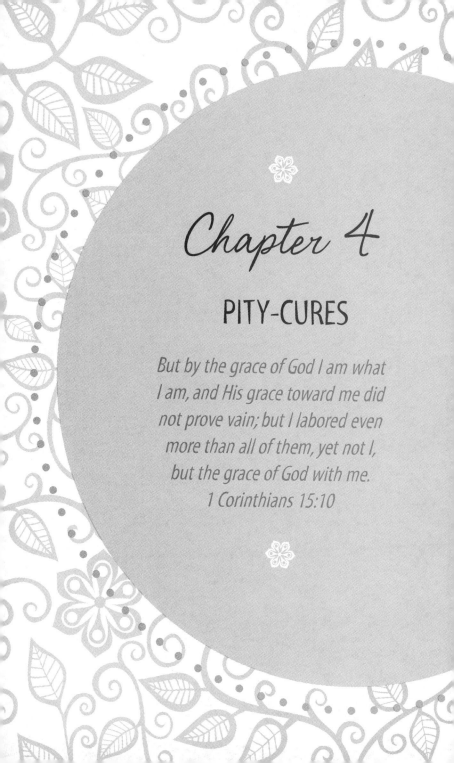

Chapter 4

PITY-CURES

*But by the grace of God I am what
I am, and His grace toward me did
not prove vain; but I labored even
more than all of them, yet not I,
but the grace of God with me.*
1 Corinthians 15:10

Some of us are natural athletes and some of us aren't. I have a friend that is faithful to exercise consistently. She puts on her little spandex outfit, pulls her hair back, and runs till she's dripping with the fruits of her labor. I often think, *Wow! That's impressive!* But it doesn't motivate me to put on my spandex. I feel like I'm doing well if I pull on a pair of sweats and do twenty minutes on the elliptical twice a week, or um. . .twice a month. Whether you are running this Christian race in fancy colored spandex or plain-Jane sweats really makes no difference. But in the book of Hebrews Paul tells us some significant strategies that will help us run the race well.

Therefore, since we are surrounded by such a huge crowd of witnesses to the life of faith, let us strip off every weight that slows us down, especially the sin that so easily trips us up. And let us run with endurance the race God has set before us. We do this by keeping our eyes on Jesus, the champion who initiates and perfects our faith.
HEBREWS 12:1–2 NLT

In my personal life I had been running the Christian race for years. I had a purpose, a focus, an urgency to move forward, no matter the cost. I stopped occasionally for rest breaks along the way, or slowed down intermittently, but steadily ran the course. However, after many years of running before that great cloud of witnesses, I sat down.

God, in His mercy, had allowed a series of personal hits to come my way, ones that had deeply wounded my inner core. I sat on the sidelines, feeling alone, unappreciated, and completely worn out. I felt like all the effort I had made had accomplished little. I *thought* I had been diligent to do the work: I had run hard, I had obeyed, I had disciplined my body for godliness—but suddenly it didn't feel like enough. I sat down to lick my wounds and pray it through. I had become tangled in a mess of sin laced with pride and self-pity.

Notice all the I's in the above description? I had a purpose. . . . All the effort I had made. . . I had been diligent. . . . I had obeyed. . . . I had been running for miles with the weight of self-sufficiency around my ankles and the sin of self-pity wrapped around my heart.

At some point in the race I had taken my eyes off Jesus and planted them right on myself. I had chosen self-pity over grace. A reading in Oswald Chambers's *My Utmost for His Highest* spoke directly into my circumstance. During my quiet time one morning, his words reminded me that circumstances will often be difficult, even painful. But we are never to give way to self-pity. If our focus is self-pity, we end up miserable and self-indulgent. We not only hinder God's provision in our own life but squelch His provision in the lives of others. Self-pity banishes the riches of God. Chambers goes on to say that there is no sin as destructive as the sin of self-pity. Self-pity annihilates God on the throne of our lives. And in His place, self-interest reigns. [11] I had done exactly what Paul had warned me not to do. Instead of stripping off sin or any thoughts and attitudes that would hinder my faith, I had embraced them. I had obliterated the grace of God and put all the responsibility on me. I took the pure gospel of Jesus off the throne and let self-worship reign.

A Christian life that consistently flows out of our own resources can become dry and purposeless. We run the race tripping over ourselves instead of resting in Jesus. We begin to serve God out of our own efforts and abilities instead of relying on the Spirit of God *in* us. Our natural abilities can easily "antagonize surrender to God." In *My Utmost for His Highest*, Chambers reminds us that holding on to our independence will invite us into the soul's most heated battle. [12] God is so utterly for our good that He will faithfully strip us of independence so that we might find the abundant life of complete dependence upon Him.

What I didn't realize is that God, in His mercy and grace, had allowed me to come to the "end" of my*self* so that I could "be met by the sufficiency of His grace." I had done all *I* could do. Most of us live our

11. Oswald Chambers, *My Utmost for His Highest* (Grand Rapids, MI: Discovery House Publishers, 1963), Feb. 6.
12. Ibid, Dec. 9.

Christian lives *conscious* of who we are and what we do. We *consciously* serve and devote ourselves to God. But Oswald Chambers says this kind of Christianity is immature and is not the abundant life Jesus speaks of. He states that the mature stage of Christianity is when we become so dependent upon God that we don't even realize we are being used. A saint that is living for God never thinks about being a saint, because he is never thinking about himself. This mature saint is so relinquished to God that consciousness of self fades away and dependence upon God reigns. [13]

This past year my husband and I did some landscaping in the backyard. One particular project involved leveling out a particular section of ground. What if on the day we had set aside to begin working, I went and got a little tin sand shovel from out of our beach bag? Then I began cutting into the sod and filling a beach bucket with my sand shovel while my husband sat pleasantly on our back deck, sipping lemonade. At times I would ask him to help give me strength and wisdom as I worked with my little shovel. Such a scenario would be entirely senseless, wouldn't it?

Now what if I told you my husband started to feel sorry for how hard I was working and decided to help out with the job? So he went and got a backhoe and came rumbling up behind me as I'm working away with

13. Ibid, Nov. 15.

my little tin shovel. Oh, I can hear you now, "Yeah, her husband came to the rescue! What a wonderful guy!" Yes, he is. I smile kindly and tell him that I appreciate his help, but I'm just fine, and I will continue to do it myself. He is welcome to park his backhoe, go back to the deck, and sit in the shade again, while sipping his lemonade. My tin shovel and I are doing just fine.

Now I know this illustration is a little ridiculous, but I think you get the point. In our daily Christian lives, instead of using the provision of the backhoe, we continue digging with our little tin shovels. Instead of using the resources of Jesus and His gospel, we let Him sit on the deck. We see ourselves as fully capable. We can do this Christian thing. We've got it down. But Christ is our sweet provision and our spiritual backhoe. As we put our lives in the seat He has provided, His strength, power, and life are manifested through us. The more we experience Christ as our resource, the more we recognize how foolish it is to keep Him in the shade. Resting in Christ-consciousness rather than living in self-consciousness puts us on the path to living abundantly *in* Him.

So if I'm made new, why would I ever choose my resources over His? Even though I have been made a new creature in my spirit, I still possess a *flesh* (or *self, self-life,* or *sinful nature,* depending on the translation used) that houses the divine nature of God.

It all began in Genesis, when Adam and Eve believed a lie over the truth. God commanded Adam: "But from the tree of the knowledge of good and evil you shall not eat, for in the day that you eat from it you will surely die" (Genesis 2:17). God's motive behind His command was good, but the enemy's *lie tempted* Eve to doubt *what God had said* (His Word) *and* to question God's motive (His heart). Satan, crafty and subtle, disguised himself and made rebellion look like innocent self-interest: "'You surely will not die! For God knows that in the day you eat from it your eyes will be opened, and you will be like God, knowing good and evil'" (Genesis 3:4–5). Eve thought it through, and then "she took from its fruit and ate" (Genesis 3:6).

Only self-interest is never innocent. Adam and Eve had a *choice* to make. Who were they going to worship: God or self? As Eve's flesh began to entertain the contorted lies of the enemy, she began to doubt what God had said. As she drew her own conclusions based on Satan's lie, she became deceived. She reached out, grabbed hold, and ate. Adam followed, choosing the lie over truth, death over life, and self over God.

In *Grace Walk*, Steve McVey describes the insignificance of good and evil to Adam and Eve before the fall. In the beginning, their focus was on God and their relationship with Him, which was God's original purpose for them. When they chose to eat of the tree of the knowledge of good and evil, their choice separated them from God. Their focus went from a God-conscious existence to a self-conscious one. Immediately they were analyzing their own "appearance, actions, and attitudes." And suddenly realized that they were naked. Instead of their focus being on God it was focused on behavior. Life no longer revolved around God. . .but around self. [14]

"But I am afraid that, as the serpent deceived Eve by his craftiness, your *minds* will be led astray from the simplicity and purity of devotion to Christ" (2 Corinthians 11:3, emphasis added). One wrong thought can start us down a path that gets us tangled in all that we are *apart* from Him. We are in Christ and we are not to live *apart* from Him any longer. In the midst of difficulty we can forget what God has said and forget who we are *in* Him. We often know better than to do that, but the subtle choice of self is so disguised it often comes unexpectedly and unannounced.

Years ago our family had invited some friends over for an evening full of summer games. An old family favorite was kick-the-can. We got an empty coffee can and set it in the middle of the front lawn. To start the game, someone is assigned to be "it" and guards the can while everyone else goes and hides. As the game begins, the "guarder" of the can ventures away little by little to see if they can find others hiding nearby. As the guarder spots the "hiders," he runs to the can, calling out their names. Those hiders are caught by the guarder of the

14. Steve McVey, *Grace Walk* (Eugene, OR: Harvest House Publishers, 1995), 110–111.

can. Other people that are still hiding can race to the can while the guarder isn't looking, and kick the can, setting free all the other hiders that had previously been caught. If that happens, the guarder counts again with closed eyes while everyone else is free to go and hide as another round begins.

This particular evening, several of the kids had been caught and were sitting on the sidelines, waiting to be set free. This competitive mom just happened to be hiding across the street in a neighbor's yard, watching all that was going on. I knew most of the players had been caught, but my strategic planning and athletic stamina could surely set them all free. I was hunched quietly behind a pine tree with my eyes planted on the guarder of the can. I just had to wait patiently for the right moment. The guarder moved back and forth, searching for more players, all the while moving farther and farther away from the can. Suddenly, I saw my chance. I bolted out from behind a pine tree and raced as fast as my short legs could carry me across the road. The cheers from the kids awaiting freedom started to ring in my ears, and I knew by now I had to have been spotted. The can was my focal point as I made the most of each stride.

Little did I know that my husband had the same plan. While I was running toward the can my husband had darted out from behind something else farther down the street. What was about to happen became a part of our family history. All I could see was the can. My eyes were dead on it. Everything else disappeared. . .until. . .my body was struck with an indescribable force. It sent my five-foot-two frame straight up in the air and spun me around like a helicopter. I remember lying on the ground, my head still spinning. My first clear thought was, *Okay, I don't think anything is broken. . . .*

I lay a while longer trying to regulate my equilibrium and gather my senses. When I opened my eyes I had about fourteen of them staring down at me. They helped me up, brushed me off, and we all had a good laugh at how competitive we can get with a can.

But that's the point. We get our eyes so focused on the *can* that we don't see clearly the lies that come with it. "I can" is one of the subtlest lies we can buy into. We fix our eyes on the *can*, the *can* will set us free, the *can* will show us we have what it takes. But that's a lie. The truth is, *we can't! It has to be Jesus! He is the only one who can!* Self-effort *can* only get us so far! The *can* won't ever reflect the glory of God no matter how resilient it might be. So, eventually God, in His grace, knocks us off our feet! He is the *can* "Guarder." He wants to protect us from the *can* that can so subtly rob us of living our life *in* Him and letting Him live His life through us.

Even though we might *choose* the *can*, God still loves and accepts us. God knew Adam and Eve would choose self over Him, and they spiritually died when they did. But if we are *in* Jesus we have a *can* guarder so that even if we foolishly choose the *can*, we won't spiritually die. It's as if God said to the enemy, "You can play the game all you want, but they're Mine now! I've filled them, sealed them, and I have My name written all over them. Even if they temporarily forget who they are, who I am, or what I've said. They might buy your lie and choose sin from time to time. But they'll never die again. They've been given eternal life in My Son, Jesus Christ."

The devil can't kill us anymore, but he is still trying to tempt us into choosing self over God in the everyday. If he can get us to feel like a worm and act like a worm, maybe we won't remember that we are butterflies. We have the same choice that Adam and Eve had that day in the garden. Although God's Spirit will creatively cause us to walk in His commands (see Ezekiel 36:27), God still gives us the freedom moment by moment to choose His way or our way. Does that mean that we don't have His redemption, grace, or identity? No! You are a butterfly and you will always be a butterfly, but you can still *choose* to *act* like a worm.

We need a second chance to see the enemy's schemes for what they really are and recognize the seriousness of our playing along! It is this flesh part of us that can be seduced into choosing independence rather than dependence on God. Eve was made in the image of God and completely void of sin when she chose to reach out and take a bite of the forbidden fruit. She was God's perfect creation tempted by the enemy's lie. That's what happened to me when I sat down from the race during that season of personal hits. I was God's perfect creation, made new in Christ, but I didn't recognize the lies. They were subtle and crafty, disguised to look like something good, and I ate. I was deceived. But over the next few months, God began to open my eyes. As the grace of second chances shone through, I saw how I had chosen to run the race apart from the Face of Grace. I was busy living my life *for* God instead of *in* Him. I was serving God in my own effort rather than resting *in Christ*. I was choosing self-worship over God-worship and independence over oneness in Him. By His grace, He was allowing me to feel the spiritual effects of my choices.

Just like in a marriage, although we can be one with our spouse, we have a choice whether or not we are going to cooperate in oneness. So it is with Jesus. We can be found *in* Him, bear His identity, and still insist on living the Christian life in our own ability. I was a butterfly and I looked like a butterfly, but I wasn't doing what a butterfly was created to do. I had forgotten I had wings. Instead of using the power and the provision of Christ *in* me to make me fly, I was running the race on my little butterfly legs, trying to do the "life of Christ" in the "power of Christ" in the "name of Christ" all in my own strength.

The flesh gratifies but never satisfies. Paul said we are to throw off what hinders us and slows us down. It isn't always big, bad, ugly sin that entangles the lives of well-intentioned Christians. An emphasis on self is as subtle and binding as an emphasis on law. For a believer in Christ who is made new, the danger of the flesh is not so much that it is evil, but that it has the ability to "seduce" us away from oneness in Christ.

In 1 Corinthians 15:10 Paul shares: "By the grace of God I am what I am, and His grace toward me did not prove vain; but I labored even more than all of them, yet not I, but the grace of God with me." Paul recognizes that despite where he came from, all that he ever was, or will be, is now marked by the grace of God. Paul sees grace as who he was *and* the foundation of everything *he* did. The grace of God was not wasted in his life; it did not prove to be empty or useless. And it wasn't even he that labored; but it was, in fact, "the grace of God with me." With the resource of God's grace *in* him, Paul knew better than to choose self to do the work. And he "labored even more than all of them"—not because Paul was so powerful but because grace was!

Jesus said, "'Apart from Me you can do nothing'" (John 15:5). Are you beginning to see why Paul "labored even more"? He lived and breathed grace so much so that he didn't have the time or reason to focus on himself. Paul rested in grace and he became "nonexistent." He lived in Christ-consciousness and left self-consciousness at the starting line. Can you imagine how much more we would accomplish as believers, moms, wives, sisters in Christ, if we would *receive, believe,* and *rest in* God's grace with bold confidence?

Like Paul, let's learn to labor in the grace of second chances. Let's try to apply this truth to our daily lives. Remember the story of Mary and Martha? The last time we saw them, Mary was sitting at the feet of Jesus. She was looking up into the face of grace, listening to the Word. She was drawing close to the heart of God, taking in the sum of God's utterances. Mary chose a position of oneness while Martha busied herself with serving. Let's review the scripture we read in chapter 1:

Now as they were traveling along, He entered a village; and a woman named Martha welcomed Him into her home. She had a sister called Mary, who was seated at the Lord's feet, listening to His word. But Martha was distracted with all her preparations; and she came up to Him and said, "Lord, do You not care that my sister has left me to do all the serving alone? Then tell her to help me." But the Lord answered and said to her, "Martha, Martha, you are worried and bothered about so many things; but only one *thing is necessary, for Mary has chosen the good part, which shall not be taken away from her."*

LUKE 10:38–42 (EMPHASIS ADDED)

Martha and Mary are a perfect picture of the difference of living *for* Christ and living *in* Christ; doing things *on our own* contrasted with doing things *in* Him. When I sat down in the race, I looked like Martha. I was "distracted . . . .worried. . .and bothered" about many things. I was *doing* the Christian life in my own strength and abilities. But Mary had chosen differently. She had chosen the *one* thing that was necessary, and Jesus said it would not be taken away. While Martha was preoccupied with serving, Mary was preoccupied with a person.

In the book *Grace Walk*, Steve McVey describes Jesus' response to Martha. He brings home the point that Jesus could have emphasized balance in serving and resting. Jesus could have said *both* were good and necessary. He could have said what Martha was doing was significant, too. But He didn't. Jesus said what Mary chose was the *one* thing that was necessary. Mary chose the good part, and Jesus was not going to take it away.[15]

What was the good part? *Oneness*. The word *one, in this verse*, (Luke 10:42) means "one in essence."[16] Through the gospel Jesus has made us one with Himself. We are in Christ and He is in us. But it is Christ's prayer in John 17 that we would choose to live out of that oneness with Him. Oswald Chambers insists that because Jesus has prayed that we might be completely *one* with Him, God will not stop moving us in that direction in honor of His Son's tender request.[17] Mary had chosen oneness with Jesus. Had Jesus asked

15. Steve McVey, *Grace Walk* (Eugene, OR: Harvest House Publishers, 1995), 39.
16. Spiros Zodiates, *The Complete Word Study New Testament* (Chattanooga, TN: AMG Publishers, 1992), Lexical Aids to the New Testament.
17. Oswald Chambers, *My Utmost for His Highest* (Grand Rapids, MI: Discovery House Publishers, 1963), May 22.

Mary to serve, I have a feeling she would have jumped up and done exactly as He asked. Her choosing to serve would have flowed out of oneness, rather than her own self-efficiency.

Although Jesus doesn't condemn Martha for her desire to serve Him, He does point out several consequences that stem from serving apart from Him; Jesus describes Martha as worried and bothered. Doesn't Martha's relationship look so much like many of ours, serving Jesus in our own strength and abilities, returning to Him when we have a specific complaint or request? Then we go off to serve again, returning when we need His help or to ask Him to bless what we are doing. Although many of us are serving wholeheartedly, we look just as worried and troubled as Martha. Does He still love us? Yes. Is His grace still sufficient? Of course. But Mary chose the one thing that is necessary: one in essence with Jesus Christ. Although God's grace was sufficient for Martha, it was Mary that could have "labored even more than all of them." It was Mary that would know grace *experientially*. It was Mary that would learn to drink deep from the river of living water and allow that river to flow into the lives of others. It is the pure gospel—Christ alone, not one tainted by works or self-effort, where the abundant life is found. Our oneness in Christ is a spiritual truth. But will we choose daily to make it our spiritual reality?

I had become so preoccupied with the Christian life that I took my eyes off *the* life. To choose oneness is to choose all that we need. To choose to grab hold of His grace is to choose to marvel at His ability to love so perfectly. To choose to live our life *in* Him is to choose to live alive. Choose grace. Wrap yourself up in its warmth, hold on to its acceptance, and move forward in its fullness every moment of every day.

Discussion Questions

1. How is grace the pity-cure?

2. Look at Hebrews 12:1–2 on page 89. What does Paul tell us to do as we run the race? What is Paul's final strategy that tells us how?

3. What is the difference between recognizing sin and focusing on sin? How does resting in God's grace take our focus from self back to Jesus?

4. What lies do you believe that cause you to doubt God's Word and His motive for your life?

5. How does the pure gospel of Jesus Christ help you kick the can in your life?

6. Can you relate more to Mary or to Martha? Can you relate more to living in Christ or living for Christ? How so?

7. What does living out of oneness with Christ look like on a daily basis? How is grace the foundation for living in oneness?

8. What does it look like to labor in grace?

9. What bird-dog truth from this chapter do you need to apply to your daily life?

Notes:

Notes:

Notes:

Notes:

Notes:

Notes:

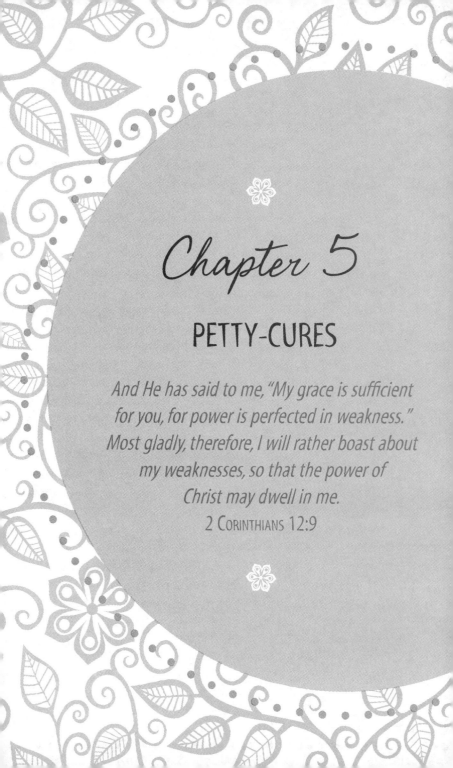

Chapter 5

PETTY-CURES

And He has said to me, "My grace is sufficient for you, for power is perfected in weakness." Most gladly, therefore, I will rather boast about my weaknesses, so that the power of Christ may dwell in me.

2 Corinthians 12:9

In *Windows on the Word,* D. H. DeHaan tells the story of a little nine-year-old boy who was struggling to practice the piano. Having found out that Ignacy Jan Paderewski, the great pianist, was coming into town to do a concert, his mother bought a ticket for her son and another for herself. The day of the concert she dressed the boy in his little tuxedo and headed for the performance. She set him down in the chair next to her and began visiting with some friends seated close by. The little boy was mesmerized with all there was to see. His eyes combed the large concert hall and then locked in on a beautiful concert grand piano on display in the center of the stage. His eyes big with enthusiasm, he felt drawn to the massive, lustrous instrument. The nine-year-old got up out of his seat and walked down the aisle, heading straight for the piano. Excitedly he crossed the stage, sat down, and began playing "Chopsticks" on the handsome keys.

As the amateur pianist's song began to echo through the great room, the spectators began to say, "Where's. . .who is. . . ?" "Hey, kid, stop!" "Where's his parents?" When the mother glanced at the stage and saw her son in all his splendor, her face turned red from embarrassment.

Standing backstage, the man of the hour, Paderewski, heard the commotion. Without the boy seeing him he came out from behind the drawn curtain and approached the piano. Upon arrival, he reached his skilled hands around the boy and joined him, improvising a lovely refrain that perfectly blended with the little boy's "Chopsticks." The boy hesitated slightly, but Paderewski spoke with wholehearted approval, "Keep it up. Don't stop. You are doing just fine."[18]

The grace of second chances extends an invitation to the people of God to encourage one another, for *His grace is sufficient* whether it needs to be applied to our weaknesses or to our sin. Even as the great Paderewski had the resources to come alongside this little one in his weakness, how much more reason do we have to come alongside each other as brothers and sisters in Christ.

Every summer our family heads up north into Canada for a camp that my husband and I help facilitate. In what is described as a spiritual boot camp for Christian teens, participants are in the Word of God six to eight hours a day, learning to study the Bible. All the activities that surround the camp are tied in to whatever truths teens are learning in the Word. Last year, one particular exercise we implemented still stands out in my memory. Let me set the stage for you. The theme for the day was "Strength in Battle." The truth we were trying to sew into the lives of the teens was that there are times in the Christian life

18. Charles Swindoll, *Swindoll's Ultimate Book of Illustrations and Quotes* (Nashville, TN: Thomas Nelson, Inc., 1998), 178.

when we need to "gird up. . .[our] mind[s]" (1 Peter 1:13 NKJV) in the midst of the battle. Spiritual, physical, and circumstantial opposition is guaranteed in the Christian life. The question is, how are we going to respond to it? Who are we going to believe?

The campers and their leaders were outside in the front yard of the lodge in a large grassy area. Female leaders were lined up on one side of the yard, facing a single-file line of girl campers. The male leaders on the other side were facing a single-file line of teen boys. The leaders were each running his or her own line of "opposition." All the female leaders stood side by side, bracing themselves in somewhat of a football stance in order to create physical opposition for the girls as they "pushed through" the center of the line of leaders, one at a time. The female leaders, myself included, who would "oppose" them silently encouraged each other as we stood in our line and awaited the teenage adrenaline that would soon be coming at us in full force.

We leaders planted our feet as firmly as possible as the "battle" began, and the first teen made her way through. We pushed our bodies against her and whispered words of opposition in her ears. As difficult as it was to speak such discouragement, we played the part well. Our words echoed familiar thoughts we have all wrestled with during battle. "You can't do it. . . ." "You give up too easily. . . . " "You don't have what it takes." The words echoed down the line as the girls fought their way through the chain of bodies in their way. Some teens fell or stumbled as they made their way along, getting up again to face the continued resistance, pushing and thrusting forward with all their might. These girls were tough; and many entered the line with stern determined faces, only to stumble through recklessly when they realized the strength of the opposition. We leaders continued to plant our feet in position, determined to create a picture of the spiritual reality we were trying to impress upon the young minds of those participating.

One by one the girls finished, tired and sore from the fight. As they completed the course, they gathered at the end of the line, cheering on those making their way through behind them. One by one, they came. One by one, they stumbled. One by one, they got back up and continued the difficult path, determined not to give up, facing opposition with courage and tenacity. As more girls got through the exercise, the sound of the cheering got louder. "Come on. . . . " "Don't give up. . . . " "You 'can do all things through Christ'. . . . " (Philippians 4:13 NKJV). The voices of encouragement slowly began to drown out the voices of the opposing side.

The last girl who came through was a natural athlete. She was strong and broad, and we leaders were getting tired. She headed in with a deadly focus, and I knew we were in for it. We ignored our aching, aging limbs and tried to give her the same strength we had given the other thirty. She pushed through the first two leaders, then stumbled as she pushed against the next two. She was up in an instant. The cheers from the back of the line were deafening. The fight was a good one, and the leaders and the teen gave each other all they had. After a steady but heated battle, she made it to the end. The roar that came out of the bodies of those girls echoed all across the camp. They had done it. They had fought and gotten through. They praised God and rallied around each other, giving hugs and hardy pats on the back. They had continued to encourage each other despite heavy and tiring opposition. And they celebrated.

As I went around loving on the girls and speaking the truth into their ears, the Holy Spirit overwhelmed me with God's heart for His people. As God brought back the hurtful words I had spoken earlier, He whispered into my heart, "Liz, that is what My children are doing to each other." It was not an audible voice that I heard but a heavy impression that moved me to tears.

There are many Christians that are stumbling forward, sometimes weakly and awkwardly, but offering their best for the kingdom of God. Often, they are running the race with endurance, serving, sharing the gospel, comforting the hurting, and taking care of their families. Not perfectly—but faithfully. Too often we miss opportunities to encourage each other and instead offer pettiness and ridicule. Rather than coming alongside each other in our weaknesses, we serve each other platters of criticism and condemnation.

Most of the time our pettiness has little to do with

the Word of God and everything to do with our own pride and self-serving desires. We choose self instead of God and man's agenda rather than God's agenda. Our motives flow from a desire to appear righteous. "Don't sing this song." "Don't pray that way." "I can't believe he used that word from the pulpit." The point is we examine things most often, not by what God has to *say* about it, but by what we *think* about it. We can use subtle and not-so-subtle maneuvers to get others to conform to our preferences. In our puffed-up spiritual critiques we appear to honor God with our lips, but our hearts are far from reflecting the heart of our God of grace.

In Mark 2:1–12, there is a story of four men who brought a paralytic to Jesus for healing. Jesus was in a home, teaching a crowd of people. Many were gathered to listen, and the crowd filled the home and flowed out through the door. "Being unable to get to Him because of the crowd, they removed the roof above Him; and when they had dug an opening, they let down the pallet on which the paralytic was lying. And Jesus seeing their faith said to the paralytic, 'Son, your sins are forgiven'" (verses 4–5).

If we imagine this story taking place today, I wonder what sort of comments would have come from the crowd listening to Jesus. While watching the paralytic's friends dig into a roof that didn't belong to them, the bystanders might have muttered, "I can't believe they are doing that!" "Who's going to pay for that?" "That isn't very Christian!" "Just who do they think they are?"

In our prideful pettiness we have a propensity to lose sight of the real thing. God's agenda gets swallowed up as we set out to prove ourselves worthy. Yet, Jesus wasn't concerned with the roof. He didn't scold the men for their insensitivity or lack of consideration. He wasn't even necessarily concerned with the physical condition of the paralytic. His main concern was for the spiritual condition of the one He had created before the beginning of time. All else became insignificant.

A man in our community recently attended a funeral for a friend. During the service the gentleman was continually distracted by a mirrored globe that hung from the ceiling in the front of the sanctuary. He was so displeased by its presence that he went back to his own church later that weekend and slandered the other church to his entire congregation. His *pettiness* kept him from experiencing *the presence*. Little did the man know that in that very funeral service, at the same time he was obsessing about the disco ball, a man who hadn't been to church for years received Christ as his personal Lord and Savior. Someone had been supernaturally snatched from the kingdom of darkness to the Kingdom of our beloved Savior, right underneath the presence of the "disco ball" of dissension.

I have a little saying I have coined to catch my own petty inclinations. It goes something like this: "Liz, it doesn't matter what *you* think, it matters what *God* thinks." That simple statement often brings quick perspective into possible petty distractions. But what gives me an even greater frame of reference is to remember how undeserving I am of God's grace covenantly entwined in me. Dwelling on the great sacrifice Jesus offered to extend grace to me, allows me the perspective I need to extend His grace to others. Who am I to be selfish when He has given so lavishly?

One time my boys were fighting over sitting in their favorite area on the couch. One of the boys pushed the other off with some unkind words and an unpleasant attitude. When I asked him why he wouldn't let his brother sit in that spot, he simply stated, "I didn't want him to." Then I said, "Would you have let me sit in that spot?" He smiled, wide-eyed, and said, "Yes, of course," as if I would be flattered by his willingness to give me his best spot. I then replied, "Why would you not extend the same grace to your brother that you would have extended to me?"

Are we being selfish with who gets our grace and how much? In Christ, God's resource of grace is abundant and in constant supply.

Does all this mean we are never to approach another believer in regard to our differences or sin in the person's life? No. Recently a friend of mine was trying to warn a young girl of her sinful choices. The girl's response was, "Stop judging me!" So I asked her, "What if you were holding a poisonous snake, and you didn't know it was poisonous? Would you want me to tell you?" To which she responded, "Of course!" Then I asked, "Would you think I was judging you?" "No,"

she said. I replied, "Precious one, you are holding a poisonous snake, and if you don't put it down you are going to get bit. That is not judging you, that is loving you."

The problem is, too often, we stand before believers and all they are holding is a stick that looks different than our stick. In our pride and self-righteousness we see their stick as a snake. In our pettiness, we set out to convince them of that "fact." But the reality is that we are seeing their stick as a snake simply because of a difference of opinion or personal preference. We then get so absorbed in allowing our own stick to define us that we end up clubbing other people with it because we are sure they are holding a snake. Funny thing happens then. Our stick turns into a snake. Did you follow that?

What might we be doing to hinder the matchless grace of God in the lives of those around us? What personal preferences might be getting in the way of the life of Christ flowing through us? Can we tell the difference between a snake and a stick? Are we able to discern God's agenda from our own?

In Matthew 7:3 Jesus reminds us to be aware of what is in our hearts when we approach others. "'Why do you look at the speck that is in your brother's eye, but do not notice the log that is in your own eye?'" Sounds a little drastic, doesn't it? Can you imagine a log coming out of your eye? It almost seems silly that Jesus would use such an exaggerated analogy to communicate our approach to others. But what He describes is profound. The other person has a speck in his eye. It is distorting his view and perhaps causing irritation in his life. But the log we have in *our* own eye communicates that we are deformed and blind. Now, Jesus uses this picture figuratively, of course. But His point is vital and meant to be heeded. Not only would we be crying out in pain and desperate for help, but there would be no chance of recouping what we have lost. Our eye is beyond repair, whereas, our brother just has a speck. We are not only to approach people in humility, remembering that we are no less guilty, but we are to approach others with a heart attitude that we are in worse shape and more desperate than they are.

Unfortunately, it often doesn't work this way. Well-meaning Christians choose self and typically throw rocks at each other, as if their way is far more righteous, perfect, or effective.

In John 8:3–11, a group of men dragged a woman out in front of Jesus. They said to Him, "Teacher, this woman has been caught in adultery, in the very act. Now in the Law Moses commanded us to stone such women; what then do You say?" (John 8:4–5).

The desire of these men was not to obey the law, or bring the woman to justice, but to trap Jesus. The Lord then knelt down to write something in the sand. The woman, most likely scared and trembling, awaited the outcome of the decision of the men surrounding her. Mosaic Law declared that as an adulteress, she should

be stoned (see Leviticus 20:10; Deuteronomy 22:22). After writing for a time, Jesus said, "'He who is without sin among you, let him be the first to throw a stone at her'" (John 8:7). Let's imagine the woman's thoughts and response:

> My head was low; I couldn't bear to look into
> their eyes. I felt naked, vulnerable, ashamed.
> If only I had chosen differently. I braced myself. . . .
> I deserved it. . . . I knew better. . . .
> I waited for the stinging stones to hit their target.
> My head still down, I anticipated my punishment. . . ,
> death surrounded me. . . ,but instead of feeling
> the sting of death. . .I heard. . .thuds. The stones were
> dropping in the dust. I must be imagining it. I lifted my
> eyes to look out from under the hair that covered my
> face. They were turning away. The men that held the
> stones were leaving. Who was this man they called
> Teacher? I raised my eyes to see Him step toward me.
> Compassion and love spilled from His eyes to mine.
> He spoke, "Woman, where did the accusers go? Didn't
> anyone condemn you?" I whispered, "Not one, sir."
> The man named Teacher responded, "Neither do I condemn
> you. You are free to go and leave your lifestyle of sin."

Jesus knew the hearts of His opponents. He didn't ignore the woman's sin nor did He deny it. She had been caught right in the middle of the act. But in the midst of the accusers Jesus took the focus from her sin to all of theirs. What Jesus revealed was not the woman's lack of sin, but the men's corrupt motives for exploiting it. Those who were in position to throw stones, were unqualified to do so. The only one who was qualified threw none. Jesus neither condoned her adultery nor did He condemn it. Jesus didn't say, "Go ahead and keep doing what you are doing." He simply said, "Go and sin no more." In other words, "Go in My grace and stop living a lifestyle of sin." Jesus extended to her the grace of second chances.

If, in the past, we have listened to modern-day Pharisees, we may find it difficult to accept God's gift of grace. Maybe your life has been full of people with impure motives who have abused their authority or used the law unlawfully to criticize and condemn you. Look into the face of grace. Jesus says, "Neither do I condemn you. 'Go and sin no more' " (John 8:11 NKJV).

We do not know what the woman did with the second chance that Jesus gave her. But we know she had a choice to make. She might have received, believed, and rested in the grace of God, or she might have chosen to go back to her old way of living. Jesus could offer her grace because that's what He came to do. He came to die on a cross, become sin for her, and rise again to fill her with His life. Do you think she took Him up on His offer, beloved? Will you?

Many of us do not know how to extend the grace of God to others because we have not fully received it for ourselves. We haven't clearly experienced the depth

of our brokenness, our desperate dependency, or the revelation of His lavish grace. We don't have the capacity to love, forgive, or extend grace unconditionally because we haven't received, believed, and rested in the truth that we are unconditionally loved and accepted by God. Jesus died to give us a new identity in Him. But we need to *believe* what God has said.

It's not just average believers who don't understand their identity in Christ. Bob George tells a story in *Classic Christianity* that challenged my own understanding of who I am in Christ. George describes a speaking engagement he had with a group of seminary students. He gave them a barrage of scenarios in order to reveal a general misunderstanding of our identity in Christ. He first asked the students if they were as "righteous and acceptable in the sight of God" as he was. George records that every hand in the room went up. He then asked them if they were as "righteous and acceptable in the sight of God as Billy Graham." In response to that question approximately half of the students raised their hands. The next question George asked challenged them to raise their hands if they considered themselves as "acceptable and righteous in the sight of God as the apostle Paul." Only about 10 percent of the hands in the room went up. George's final question to the group of seminary students was a big one. He boldly asked, "How many of you in the sight of God are as righteous and acceptable as Jesus Christ?" George's point was made. Three lone hands were raised in the midst of an auditorium filled with seminary students.[19]

In Christ, we are completely acceptable and righteous in the sight of God. God took our sins at the cross two thousand years ago and put them on Jesus. Then God took the righteousness of Jesus and put it on us. He exchanged Jesus' life for ours, our sin for His righteousness. "He made Him who knew no sin to be sin on our behalf, so that we might become the righteousness of God *in* Him" (2 Corinthians 5:21, emphasis added). Many of us have the idea of grace in our heads, but my prayer is that we might *know* the revelation of His grace in our hearts. How can we even begin to declare ourselves righteous and acceptable in God's eyes? Is it because of what we do? Never! It is only because of who we are *in* Jesus Christ.

If Jesus is your Savior, then you are *in* Him: fixed, enveloped, surrounded, covenantly entwined with His grace—you are completely righteous and acceptable to God! If you have a hard time believing this truth, begin to say it out loud to yourself. Practice the skills of a good bird dog, and seek this truth amid all the lies, distractions, and difficulties of daily life.

We receive grace, our identity in Christ, and Christ's righteousness—by faith in Jesus Christ. When we see the extent of the matchless grace of God, when we stand at the base of the oak tree and see its vastness, when we begin to absorb how priceless the gift, when

19. Bob George, *Classic Christianity* (Eugene, OR: Harvest House, 1989), 92–93.

we finally begin to see the warmth and power of grace and how lavishly God gives it to us, how can we not be compelled to extend it to others?

Discussion Questions

1. Are you known as an encourager in the body of Christ? Why or why not?

2. How have you let your own pettiness or agenda get in the way of extending grace to others?

3. Can you tell the difference between a snake and a stick? What sticks do you sometimes confuse as a snake?

4. Have you ever used your stick to club others? Is there anyone from whom you need to ask forgiveness for your lack of grace?

5. Do you tend to be a rock thrower or a rock dropper? How can a revelation of God's grace keep you from picking up a rock at all?

6. Do you see yourself as completely righteous in the sight of God? Do you see other believers as completely righteous in the sight of God?

7. Read 2 Corinthians 12:9, and then make a list of your weaknesses. How is God's grace sufficient for each one? What about the weaknesses of your spouse, children, or other believers in your life?

8. Has the truth of the grace of second chances made its way into your heart, or is it more of a concept stuck in your head? Do you believe God?

9. What bird-dog truth from this chapter do you need to apply to your daily life?

Notes:

Notes:

Notes:

Notes:

Notes:

Notes:

....

....

....

....

....

....

....

....

....

....

....

....

....

....

....

....

....

....

....

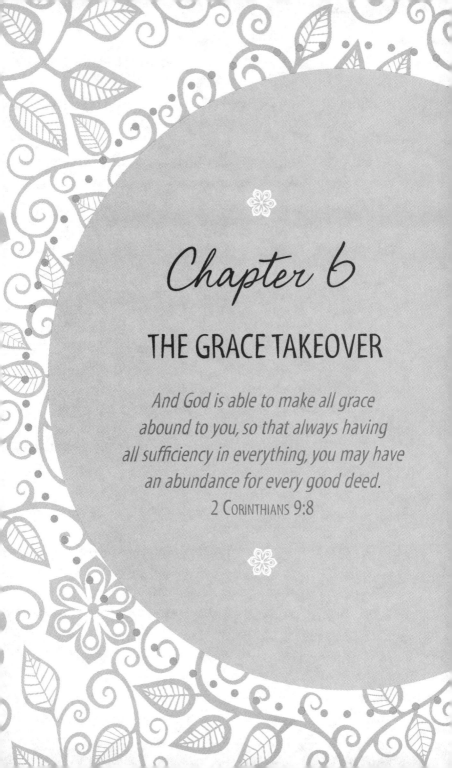

Chapter 6

THE GRACE TAKEOVER

*And God is able to make all grace
abound to you, so that always having
all sufficiency in everything, you may have
an abundance for every good deed.*
2 Corinthians 9:8

Few things will change a life as much as a first-born baby. There are months of preparing, planning, and productivity. Hours are spent decorating a nursery and going to numerous doctor appointments. Conversations, even with perfect strangers, revolve around the growing bulge in your middle. Suddenly everyone feels entitled to comment on how you look and feels free to touch your belly. Unwarranted parenting advice flows freely.

Then there is the delivery, and you finally bring the baby home. At that moment you realize that nothing turns the world upside down like this beautiful, big-eyed, bald-headed, milk-slurping miracle. Change is inevitable with late-night feedings and intentional glimpses at the small tummy that slowly rises up and down with each tiny breath. With the first glance at that pink, furrowed face your heart is forever different. Within that pint-sized, blameless, bundle of joy lies the capacity to experience a sense of awe you never knew existed. How can something so seemingly small and vulnerable take over life in such monumental proportions?

And so it is with grace. Grace, up close and personal, has the capability to transform a life. Grace should change the way we do things. It should change the way we see things. Whether we are aware of it or not, grace changes who we are. It has the miraculous ability to turn our "Christian" lives upside down and inside out. As we open the gift of grace, we are invited to live a depth of life we never knew existed. When something takes us over, it rules us. Purpose, perspective, and provision are never the same again.

This gift of grace that Jesus extends toward those who love Him is meant to change us. It is meant to take over. As a legalist, I gauged the success of my Christian life on my behavior. I was bound up in sin management, focused on accomplishing Christianity in my own strength and striving to obey God. As I examined God's gift of grace more closely, God showed me that I had been swinging on a religious pendulum of performance. When I did something right, the pendulum would sway far left. I was pleased that I had obeyed God and found favor with Him. The right side was the side of grace. When I needed forgiveness I would swing to the right and tap into the grace God offered me in Christ. The grace side of the pendulum was a place I would go when I missed it, messed up, or didn't measure up. I would swing left doing it right and then swing right when I did it wrong. Left and right, back and forth, dipping into God's grace when my attempts to do the Christian life fell short. It was a relationship with Christ based on performance and self-mastery. Grace became a bandage that covered my sin when I messed up, rather than an outpouring of the radical acceptance of God.

What God showed me is how we cheapen His grace and His gospel when we swing back and forth on a pendulum of any kind. I am to stay put in Christ. I am to find a home there. I am not to just *think* the truth, *say* the truth, or *hear* the truth. But *receive, believe,* and *rest in* the truth that His grace is indeed, sufficient. I am to allow grace to turn my Christian world upside down. Takeover grace is meant to hold us—stable, fixed, and established in the atonement of Jesus Christ.

We need to be a "good bird dog" and seek out the lavish supply of grace as we live out our life *in* Christ: "And God is able to make *all GRACE abound* to you, so that *always* having *all* sufficiency in *everything*, you may have an *abundance* for *every* good deed" (2 Corinthians 9:8, emphasis added). Did you catch the sufficiency of His grace? Do you see the endless provision of takeover grace? There is no lack. As deep as you go and as far as you see, His grace is there. "For as high as the heavens are above the earth, so great is His lovingkindness toward those who fear Him. As far as the east is from the west, so far has He removed our transgressions from us" (Psalm 103:11–12).

We are fixed *in*, enveloped *in*, surrounded *in* an ocean of boundless grace. Not based on our goodness, but on His. Wave upon wave of divine kindness, favor, and acceptance surround us. In every direction we look, there is nothing but whitecap after whitecap of the grace of second chances lapping up against us. From horizon to horizon, as far as we can see, the depth of

God's radical acceptance whispers to His chosen ones. Gaze once again into the vastness of His grace. It is meant for you, and it was meant to take over.

Paul said to the Galatians, "It was for freedom that Christ set us free; therefore keep standing firm and do not be subject again to a yoke of slavery" (Galatians 5:1). Slave yokes were heavy and binding and designed to hold a slave captive. The yoke would lie across the slave's shoulders inhibiting movement and oppressing freedom. In chapters 3 and 4 we talked about the most common barriers to the grace of second chances. Some of us have possibly worn a yoke of law or self-worship for so long we don't even recognize the burden of it. In an ocean of grace, the slave yoke will most certainly cause us to struggle. Imagine frantically treading water, burdened by a heavy yoke of slavery that Christ took off our shoulders long ago. We struggle, trying to keep our heads up and our lives afloat, all the while surrounded by an ocean of amazing grace.

One night many years ago I heard a struggle going on in my little boy's room. I got out of bed and made my way down the hall. There he was, face down on his bed, kicking his legs and thrashing his arms wildly. I called his name, but he didn't answer. I thought something was terribly wrong. I crossed the room, still saying his name aloud, and placed my hand on the small of his twisting back. He was sound asleep, lost in an obviously disturbing dream. When I finally got him awake he told me that he had dreamt he had fallen into the water. Although I was relieved after hearing a simple explanation for the ordeal, I was enchanted at the vigor with which he had fought while in the midst of the dream. Because the dream seemed so real, it had warped his perception of what was true. He had no recollection that amid the struggle, he had been safe all along.

We do the same thing in our Christian lives. There are many of us that are struggling under the weight of a yoke other than the one Jesus offers. Why? Because we forget that we have been eternally *made over*. We forget that we are *in* Him. And we forget that we are surrounded and saturated with *boundless* grace. When we forget the truth of who we are and *whose* we are, we can be overcome with wrong perceptions.

Many of us Christians struggle with consciously and consistently standing firm in the grace of second chances. Instead, we unknowingly swing back and forth on the pendulum of performance-based religion. This subtle, self-focused ride is inhibiting Christ in us, weighing us down, and oppressing the abundant life Jesus promised. It keeps us thrashing in our own efforts instead of *resting* in the atonement of Jesus Christ. He freed us to fill us. He wants to live His life through us. And He has strategically placed us in an ocean of lavish grace so that our focus can be on Him, for His name, and His gospel. Live in Him and float free.

Are you ready for takeover grace? Are you ready

to shed the yoke of slavery, beloved of God? Are you tired of treading water in an attempt to do what Christ has already done? Let's give up striving, sulking, and self-sufficiency and *rest* in the One on whom we are completely dependent.

Any mother who has had little ones knows what it is to have tiny hands clinging to a skirt or pant leg while trying to work unhindered. No matter how she might distract them, they are typically bound and determined to remain at her feet. They are ever present, grasping, grunting, and pulling, with eyes fixed on the one they cling to. If too much time passes, the pulls get stronger and the grunts get louder.

When my boys were little, they never would have crawled over to the corner, sulking if I didn't pick them up. They wouldn't have retreated with a heart that said, "She doesn't love me" or "I'm not good enough." As a child longs for recognition, his heart is whispering, "I want you. You are my world, the source of all that I need." Children are completely comfortable with being completely dependent. In fact, at that age, they wouldn't have it any other way. In order to know takeover grace, our spiritual position needs to resemble a toddler at his mother's heels. We need to grow completely comfortable with being completely dependent.

Absolute dependence upon God is what lands us in a yoke of takeover grace that leads to rest. Many of us think a week at the beach, some Christian retreat, or a nap in a hammock is rest. The "rest" Jesus speaks of is an internal rest, not an external one.

Jesus says, "'Come to Me, all who are weary and heavy-laden, and I will give you rest. Take My yoke upon you and learn from Me, for I am gentle and humble in heart, and YOU WILL FIND REST FOR YOUR SOULS. For My yoke is easy and My burden is light'" (Matthew 11:28–30). The Message translates these verses this way:

> *"Are you tired? Worn out? Burned out on religion? Come to me. Get away with me and you'll recover your life. I'll show you how to take a real rest. Walk with me and work with me—watch how I do it. Learn the unforced rhythms of grace. I won't lay anything heavy or ill-fitting on you. Keep company with me and you'll learn to live freely and lightly."*

Jesus says to know *real rest* is to *come to Him*. He invites us to take the yoke that He offers. Resting in Christ doesn't mean ceasing from all activity. It means ceasing from activity that has its origin in us. The yoke Jesus described was a curved piece of wood that was fitted around the neck of two oxen, used to pull a plow. The picture Jesus illustrates is an invitation to be yoked together, with Christ as the lead "ox." When we choose to be yoked with Christ, we are bound together. Notice, our part lies in *coming* to Him and *taking* His yoke. To respond to Jesus' invitation requires action, not simply intent. Then He asks us to do the following: to "keep company" with Him; our walking and working is to be *with* Him, learning "the unforced rhythms of grace," living "freely and lightly." Quite a different picture than the heavy, binding, inhibiting yoke of slavery. Isn't it? So, how are we to *do* the yoke of Jesus? In our own ability and effort? No, we do this by *resting* in takeover grace.

In ballroom dancing, the man is to lead. The woman's job is to put her hand in his and line up with him. She has studied and gotten to know her partner. She has learned to read his expressions and sense his movement. She follows each well-placed step. As he moves, she moves. She leans into him as if to get a better sense of where he will go next. All of her is tuned into him. He does the work, and she rests as she labors, trusting his guidance. The skilled leader bears the responsibility of their placement on the floor and the rhythm of their movement. He feels her reliance upon him and leads with gentle confidence, knowing it is his job to make a way for her. They are yoked together, moving in the same direction with the same purpose.

We will learn the yoke of Christ and the unforced rhythms of grace as we learn to rest in the strength and power of the pure gospel of Jesus Christ. We follow His lead. Where He goes, we go. When He veers left, we veer left. Our job is not to look down the path or worry about the obstacles in the way but to tune in to His leading. We are to rest in His yoke. We are to find a home there. It is a place of security, relief, and oneness.

For any of you who thought there was more to the Christian life than what you have found, come to Him, put on His yoke, and enter into His rest. He invites us to dance, moment-by-moment, day-by-day, to the unforced rhythms of grace.

If we were completely honest with ourselves, it is much more difficult and takes far more courage to surrender to God's moment-by-moment provision of grace than to live in the provision of our own strength. It is much easier to dance our own dance than to learn to glide with our beloved Savior. To abandon all to Christ, is to give in to resting, trusting, and believing. It feels vulnerable. It is to abandon independence and be desperate for dependence upon Him. It is to unclench our hands and let go of all we have been dying to hold on to and open them, palms up, to the one who died for us.

Real rest in Jesus has less to do with our circumstances and more to do with our relationship with Him. The amount we trust Him will directly correlate to the rest we experience. In most cases it is easier to serve God than to love Him. We fear giving up control and are afraid to grow close and dependent. So we live Christianity at a distance from the very One who gave us His life. Jesus has created us, sustained us, and established us in Himself. Look up into the Face of Grace. He longs to love you freely and for you to offer your love freely to Him.

In his book *Holiness*, J. C. Ryle writes that pride and unbelief are still stuck in the hearts of believers, causing many of us to continue to keep living our lives at a distance from Jesus. Ryle states we are blind to the enormity of the debt Jesus paid on our behalf and feel no great debt of gratitude to Him in response. Few of us realize our daily need for Him or how free we are to hang on Him as a child hangs on a parent. Many of us don't understand how fully He loves His people. How Jesus delights in meeting every weakness and inadequacy. We don't realize the anguish of His love or His passionate desire to reach out and save His own. There is nothing Christ desires more than a needy people willing to lean into Him, to rest in Him, and cry out to Him. [20]

The origin of our love for God begins with an enduring awareness of God's love for us. As we willingly open our hearts to be loved by God, our love for Him will increase. "We love, because He first loved us" (1 John 4:19). Many of us haven't learned to trust God because we don't really know Him. Let Him delight in you, beloved. Much of our love for Jesus will flow out of our ability to enjoy His love for us. Some of the wisest words ever spoken to me were from a grace-filled teacher. He said, "Liz, enjoy God enjoying you." Those simple, undemanding words gave me a step up in learning takeover grace. To enjoy God brings us close. To allow Him to enjoy us draws us even closer.

Watch out! When we allow ourselves to enjoy Him

20. J. C. Ryle, *Holiness* (ReadaClassic.com, 2010), 276.

and let Him enjoy us, when we drop our arms of self-protection and let all our defenses fall to the ground, when we stop holding back and instead, open up, we fall head over heels in love with Jesus. His yoke becomes comfortable, easy, and light, and we enter into His rest. It's not that we won't ever come out from under the yoke or never struggle with some of life's challenges. But as our walk with Jesus becomes more consistently dependent, it will become more consistently joyful, grace-filled, and life-giving.

Jesus says, "Will you believe what I have said? Will you walk, live, and rest in your eternal makeover? Will you trust Me enough to let Me live My life through you?" He longs for you, beloved of God. You are His delight! Will you look up into the Face of Grace and let Him saturate you with the reality of His abundant, perfect love? Will you let His gift of takeover grace go from a concept to a reality in your life?

To let God love on us requires an intentional, simple faith. Not a faith that is found once and tucked away, but an active faith that is offered in the everyday. Not a huge, bold, takeover faith that we would expect to be the requirement of a surrendered life, but a pure faith offered in childlike trust. So how much faith does it take? How does a woman of God learn to live in takeover grace? One mustard seed of faith at a time.

Faith, the size of a mustard seed, will move mountains (see Matthew 17:20). One mustard seed of faith offered again and again over the course of a day can move our dry Christian life into mountain-moving adventures. The simplicity of our part stuns me. Jesus simply asks us to believe Him and then invites us to rest in what He has accomplished. " 'It is finished!' " (John 19:30). Jesus has done it all. He simply invites us to choose Him, moment by moment, step-by-step, trial by trial, grace upon grace. He has done the work; our job is to surrender.

At church one Sunday morning, a little girl grabbed the offering plate that was being passed and put it on the floor. To her parent's surprise, the little girl stepped into the plate and stood up straight and tall. The usher asked, "Sweetheart, what are you doing?" To which the little girl responded, "I'm giving Jesus all of me!"

To the little girl, the act of surrendering to Jesus was a no-brainer. She didn't make it complicated, analyzing it with a bunch of "what ifs" or "whys." She didn't let her eyes fall on her own inadequacies or question the plan. She just saw who Jesus was, stepped forward in faith, and gave Him her all. Jesus doesn't need us all polished up and pretty; He doesn't want our perfection, service, or our sacrifice. First and foremost, Jesus simply wants us! Just as we are!

Takeover grace begins with our decision to do exactly what that little girl did, every moment of every day. Christ desires a simple faith to see Him as He is and then step forward and rest in all that He has *done*! " 'Come to Me. . .and I will give you rest' " (Matthew 11:28). We offer up all that we are, and He offers us takeover grace.

Hebrews 10:14 states, "For by that *one offering* he *forever made perfect* those who are being made holy" (NLT, emphasis added). Jesus offered Himself on the cross, one time, two thousand years ago, and one offering perfected forever all those who belong to Him! Beloved, that is a bird-dog truth worthy of getting ahold of! That is takeover grace wanting to take over your heart! There was one offering, for all the trillions and trillions of sins, by millions and millions of believers, all over the world, for thousands and thousands of years, since the beginning of the human race. Every stain and offense, every evil thought, condemning attitude, any and every contamination of the human soul. . .perfected. Once. . .for. . .all!

The Word of God says that we have been made perfect. Not because of who *we* are but because of who *He* is. We don't need to get better and stronger at doing Christianity. We need to get better and stronger at letting *Him* do it through us.

The rest of walking with Jesus comes when we take one step at a time. Instead of using all our efforts to do it right, we can use all of our effort to do it at rest. Instead of working in self-sufficiency, we can labor in Christ-sufficiency. Instead of mustering up every ounce of strength to be perfect, we can surrender every weakness and His strength is perfected. Instead of planning all the details, we can purpose to trust them to Him. Instead of trying to be holy, we can rest in the One who is holy. Instead of living our life for Him, we can live our life *in* Him. Instead of us tapping into grace, we can let grace take over.

No matter how we describe the God of second chances, our words will always fall short. To try to explain Him is beyond our human vocabulary. What human being can even begin to substantially illustrate God's great love, holiness, or kindness? If every mouth were to utter His name, and every knee were to bow in submission, and every song of praise were to be sung at once, we would still not come close to accurately communicating the awesomeness of God. His glory, power, and goodness go further still. And so it is with grace.

Maybe it's a little hard for us to believe that God just wants to love us. His message of grace is from God's heart to ours. The Bible tells us that His grace "is sufficient" (2 Corinthians 12:9), that God is "the God of all grace" (1 Peter 5:10), and that through Jesus we have "received. . .grace upon grace" (John 1:16). Wave upon wave of graces washes us each and every day. God's own signature of grace is woven on the fibers of our being. It is through grace that oneness, rest, and radical acceptance flow. Most of us have only just begun to recognize the shadow of the real thing—what "it" looks like, acts like, smells like. We try desperately to fit grace into a box or define it with brilliant theological terms and creative illustrations. But the more I look into the gift of grace, bask in its vastness, and am washed in its waves, the more my eyes are opened to its life-giving power. As I realize more and more how uncontainable it is, the more clearly I understand that grace is not an "it." Grace isn't simply a doctrine, a principle, or an ideology. Grace is a person. Ultimately, grace is not something to be discovered, sought, or found, but received. It is a gift, a free gift, and there is really only one word that truly encapsulates the mystery of God's lavish grace: Jesus.

Discussion Questions

1. Discuss the statement: "Grace became a bandage that covered my sin when I messed up, rather than an outpouring of the radical acceptance of God." Can you relate to what the author is describing? Why or why not?

2. How do we cheapen God's grace and His gospel when we swing back and forth on a religious pendulum of performance?

3. Which phrase best describes your Christian life: sin management or dancing to the "unforced rhythms of grace"? Why would so many of us rather dance our own dance? What are the lies we believe when we do?

4. What does takeover grace look like to you? Meditate on 2 Corinthians 9:8. Replace the "you" in the verse with your name. Do you live like that grace is available to you?

5. How does your relationship with God correlate with your ability to enter into His rest?

6. Have you stood in the offering plate and offered all of yourself to Jesus? Do you hold back from God? If so, what do you hold back? Why or why not?

7. Write Hebrews 10:14 on an index card, and place it where you will be able to see it. Daily meditate on the truth that you have already been perfected in Christ.

8. Do you believe, when it's all said and done, that God just wants to love you? Are you afraid to let Him love you? Why or why not?

9. What bird-dog truth stands out in this chapter, one that you can begin to meditate on and "sew" into your daily life?

Notes:

Notes:

Notes:

Notes:

Notes:

Notes:

Conclusion

There is a story of a father and his son riding on a wagon across the prairie. It had been a long hot day, and they were on their way home for dinner. Far off in the distance the father spotted smoke rising against the horizon. It was a raging grass fire moving rapidly across the flat prairie. The father snapped the reins, and the horses took off in an attempt to outrun the flames that were heading their way.

After a short distance the father realized they were running out of time. The fire was approaching far too quickly. He pulled the wagon over and jumped out. He gave orders to his son, and they began to dig a small ditch. Then the father set fire to the grass in a circle around him, his son, and the wagon. He burned as big a space as time allowed. The prairie fire raged as it advanced toward them.

"Father, we have to get away from here!" the son screamed.

"No, Son. . .stand."

"Dad, it's too hot and it's too big!"

"Trust me, Son. You need to stand."

"Dad, we are almost out of time, we need to run."

"No, Son. The only thing you need to do is trust me . . .and stand."

"Dad, how can I stand when there is fire all around me?"

"Son, I already burned the grass where you stand. It was set on fire. What would normally burn is already dead. It is finished. The fire can come close but it won't touch us. Trust me. . .and stand."[21]

Beloved, we stand in Christ. No matter how big the fire gets, no matter how hot life becomes, Christ has already made a way. In Christ, *all* is already accomplished. Through grace, we have *all* of Him in us, not just part of Him. We have *all* the atonement of Jesus Christ, not just part of it. Living in that safe place is a matter of us resting in His *all-ness*. No matter what kind of fire it is. Until we see Christ as in *all* and through *all*, we will always be tempted to make it happen ourselves. Growing in Christ doesn't mean perfectly getting our act together; it means recognizing that we are completely perfect *in* Him. As believers, we can stop crucifying ourselves. We have already died with Christ. Christ died once. . .for *all* (see Hebrews 9:28; 1 Peter 3:18). Those in Christ stand in *the* safe place. We need only trust Him.

His grace is sufficient, His love unsurpassed, His

21. Tony Evans, *Tony Evans' Book of Illustrations* (Chicago, IL: Moody Publishers, 2009), 259.

sacrifice more than enough. When all of life shakes down, when flesh is completely stripped away, when every deed is recorded and every knee bowed, the atonement of Christ still stands. The gift of the grace of second chances is more profound than we will ever know.

If you have come to the end of this book and you still have not made *the* Jesus Christ *your* Jesus Christ, this is a second chance to do so. Jesus hung on a cross so long ago to pay for the sin of the world. Through His grace, He offers you payment for your sins, all of Himself, and His life in you. Would you receive the invitation to make the God of second chances your deliberate choice? He is *all*, and He is *all* you will ever need.

About the Author

Elizabeth Ward spends her time teaching the Word of God, counseling, writing, and loving on her family. She is a writer for Circle of Friends Ministries and a contributing author in the Circle of Friends devotionals, *Shared Blessings* and *A Place to Belong.*

Acknowledgments

Thank You—Father, Son, and Holy Spirit. I am enamored with You. The mystery of Your love and grace astound me. Every breath, every day, every relationship You bless me with is a constant unveiling of Your glorious grace in my life. To know You is to only long for more.

Shawn, you are my hero. I am so blessed to do life with you in the name of Jesus. Thank you for all you have sacrificed and for the grace you continually extend to me. This project is as much yours as anyone's. I love you.

To my sons Jarod, Rylan, and Seth. Thank you for the extra weight you have pulled and the "convenience" food you have eaten while Mom took time to write. I love you like crazy! May you fall ferociously in love with Jesus and live passionately in His grace, unapologetically. I can't imagine how much God delights in you! My cup overflows!

Thank you to my parents, in-laws, and siblings. Each one of you has been so faithful to love me well, even in the midst of my weaknesses. So glad we have eternity to continue the adventure we've begun. I can't wait to see Him face-to-face.

Thank you, Janine, Rachele, and Jocelyn. You are more than sisters, you are my dearest friends. God knew what He was doing when He gave me each of you. Your hearts are stunningly beautiful.

Thank you to all those who have contributed in

faithful prayer and encouragement: Lillian, Bobby, Katie, Kim, Pam, Kristi, Deb, and so many others. It means more than you know, and I am forever grateful. Thanks, too, for all those at GCC who have invested in growing me up in the grace and knowledge of Jesus Christ. I am richly blessed!

Thanks to Kristin and all my co-laborers for the gospel at TFC, for your unrelenting pursuit of God, your constant prayers, and for consistently extending to me the grace of second chances. It has been an honor running the race with you.

Thank you to my sisters at Circle of Friends— Jocelyn, Tanya, Lisa, and Missy—for the prayers, encouragement, laughter, expertise, and opportunity to walk alongside you wherever He calls. You are such a precious group of women.

Thank you to Kelly McIntosh, Linda Hang, and the rest of the team at Barbour Publishing for your investment in the Kingdom and the compilation of this project. To God be the glory!

What Is Circle of Friends?

Circle of Friends Ministries, Inc. (COF) is a nonprofit organization established to build a pathway for women to come into a personal relationship with Jesus Christ and to build Christian unity among women. Our mission is to honor Jesus Christ through meeting the needs of women in our local, national, and international communities. Our vision is to be women who are committed to Jesus Christ, obediently seeking God's will, and fulfilling our life mission as Christ-followers. As individuals and as a corporate group, we minister a Christ-centered hope, biblically based encouragement, and unconditional love by offering God-honoring, Word-based teaching, worship, accountability, and fellowship to women in a nondenominational environment through speaker services, worship teams, daily web blogs and devotionals, radio programs, and GirlFriends teen events.

COF also partners with churches and women's groups to bring conferences, retreats, Bible studies, concerts, simulcasts, and servant evangelism projects to their communities. We have a Marketplace Ministry that teaches Kingdom principles in the workplace and are committed to undergirding, with prayer and financial support, foreign mission projects that impact the world for Jesus Christ. Our goal is to evangelize the lost and edify the body of Christ by touching the lives of women—locally, nationally, and globally. For more information, visit www.ourcircleoffriends.org.